THE KETO INSTANT POT® COOKBOOK

The Keto Instant Pot®
COOKBOOK

KETOGENIC DIET PRESSURE COOKER
RECIPES MADE EASY & FAST

Urvashi Pitre

Photography by Hélène Dujardin

ROCKRIDGE
PRESS

For general information on our other products and services or to obtain technical support, please contact our Customer Care Department within the U.S. at (866) 744-2665, or outside the U.S. at (510) 253-0500.

Rockridge Press publishes its books in a variety of electronic and print formats. Some content that appears in print may not be available in electronic books, and vice versa.

Photography © Hélène Dujardin
Food styling by Tami Hardeman
Author photo © John Kasinger

Interior design by Lisa Schneller-Bieser

ISBN: Print 978-1-64152-043-0 | eBook 978-1-64152-044-7
Printed in Canada

To my mother, Major Veena Pitre, a decorated army officer, successful business woman, best-selling author, healer, and inspiration to many. She was a woman well-ahead of her times, and taken from us all too soon.

Thanks, Mom, for forcing me to learn how to cook, putting up with me complaining about it daily, yet never letting up on me. I miss you every day.

CONTENTS

INTRODUCTION

When I was 20 years old, I came to this country alone, with two suitcases, $20, and the promise of a scholarship. Since then, I've almost died two separate times. I've been wheelchair bound for months. I've had to learn how to walk again. I rose to the rank of Chief Marketing Information Officer (CMIO) for the largest ad agency in this country. And I created a multimillion-dollar business from scratch.

None of this was as hard as losing weight.

I struggled for 10 years, did everything I knew how to do, tried almost every diet, and yet I just could not lose weight and keep it off.

If you are ever about to be stranded on a desert island, you should pick me to be your companion. Not just because I would be wonderful company—witty and charming as I am—but because I can apparently survive and gain weight on hardly any food at all! You could eat everything in sight, guilt-free, and not have to watch me waste away.

I hated being overweight. I knew that when people looked at me, they assumed I was fat because I ate a lot and because I had no self-control. Nothing could have been further from the truth: I ate little, I starved myself, and I am a control freak with few self-control issues. What I do have is a metabolism that is extremely carbohydrate sensitive.

As I said, I tried almost every diet—everything except low-carb and keto. I am a reluctant carnivore (which, by the way, is a great name for a band). I couldn't fathom eating as much meat as a low-carb diet would necessitate. But after 10 years of failing, I decided to have gastric sleeve surgery. I had to accept that I would have to eat a low-carb keto diet because the surgery alone would not be enough. You can cut most of your stomach out, but if you still eat carbs and are carb sensitive, you will neither keep all the weight off nor stay slim.

My husband decided to join me. Between us, we had 180 pounds to lose. Thus began our journey four years ago, which was the genesis of my blog, TwoSleevers.com. I started to blog recipes as I learned how to cook delicious, easy, low-carb meals.

It is one thing to make delicious food. It is another to be able to make it easier. Enter the Instant Pot®. With its ability to cook meats in a hurry, to infuse flavors from pressure cooking, and to allow hands-off cooking, the appliance began to play a greater part in my cooking.

I wrote this book to help people like me enjoy delicious foods that are easy to make. One thing that is essential for us on the keto diet: We must switch away from the mind-set of all the foods we can't have to focus on those we can have. Meats, cheeses, butter, bacon, vegetables, nuts—the list goes on and on! I've tried to create recipes that everyone in your family will enjoy, with few specialty ingredients. That way, you can make these dishes and feed everyone in your family the same food. Keto may be considered a "special diet," but it doesn't have to be limiting and difficult. This cookbook gives you proof of that.

1

Keto Made Easy

I wish someone had told me the one simple principle I needed to understand the mechanics of weight loss. Here it is: Your body is either releasing insulin or it's not. If it's releasing insulin, you're not burning fat. That's literally all I needed to know. Everything else about weight loss and the ketogenic diet focuses on the details of how to keep your insulin levels low:

■ You restrict carbs because carbs cause you to release insulin.

■ You eat moderate amounts of protein because excess protein can cause you to release insulin.

■ You eat more fat because fat does not cause you to release insulin.

■ You pair the ketogenic diet with intermittent fasting and/or no grazing between meals to reduce insulin secretion and increase insulin sensitivity.

This is the big picture. I go through the details on the following pages before jumping into the beautiful marriage of the Instant Pot® and the keto diet.

KETO BASICS

The ketogenic (keto) diet is based on a normal metabolic process called "ketosis," which happens when your body does not have enough glucose for energy, and therefore burns fat instead. During ketosis, chemical molecules called "ketones" are produced in the liver when the fat is burned, and they are sent into your bloodstream to be used as fuel for the brain, muscles, and tissues. Ketosis was likely a process that allowed humans thousands of years ago to survive when carbohydrates were not readily available for long stretches of time. The keto diet deliberately reduces carbohydrate intake to encourage the body to burn fat instead.

Macronutrients

Reaching ketosis is not as simple as just cutting your carb consumption down and eating more fat. It is more precise and requires careful balancing of your macronutrients (macros)—fat, protein, and carbohydrates. The keto diet is a low-carb, moderate-protein, and high-fat plan, which usually breaks down into the following percentages daily:

- 60 to 75 percent of calories from fat

- 15 to 30 percent of calories from protein

- 5 to 10 percent of calories from carbs

Every single meal does not have to be in perfect balance, but the proportions should be close to these at the end of the day.

Setting the Right Macros for You

Everyone has unique keto macros to produce the desired effects, such as weight loss or maintenance, depending on height, weight, goals, exercise level, and body fat percentage. This is why using an online keto calculator can be very effective for figuring out your individual dietary needs. These calculators can calculate your macro numbers and daily calorie count to keep you in the state of ketosis, or get you there initially. Since carbohydrates (glucose) are the usual primary fuel source for the body, it is important to stay within the recommended macro range when considering your food choices. If your carbs are too high, you will not reach ketosis at all.

For more than two years, I have tracked my intake carefully and obsessively. After a lot of experimenting, I know what works for me. I started the journey at 5 feet, 5 inches tall and 230 pounds. My goal weight was 152 pounds, which I reached over 10 interminable, difficult months. To achieve weight loss, I had to eat less than 800 calories per day and keep carbs between 20 and 25 grams. For maintenance, I can eat 1,200 to 1,300 calories per day and keep carbs between 50 and 75 grams. I still gain when I consume 80 grams of carbs or more per day. To lose a small regain in weight now, I have to fast intermittently every other day and restrict carbs to 20 to 30 grams per day until the gain is gone. Knowing this has helped me maintain my weight over the past three years.

I taught myself how to follow the keto diet by consulting three sources:

- *The Obesity Code: Unlocking the Secrets of Weight Loss,* by Jason Fung

- *Why We Get Fat: And What to Do About It,* by Gary Taubes

- *The Art and Science of Low Carbohydrate Living,* by Jeff S. Volek and Stephen D. Phinney

These sources provide the scientific rationale and research that underlie their recommendations, which I appreciate.

Low-Carb Food Choices

Although the carb amount we consume each day is low, we still get to choose where those carbs come from for our meals and snacks. You will be looking mostly at net carbs, the total grams of carbs minus the grams of fiber, as a guideline for reaching the right amount of carbs for your body.

The recipes in this book, for the most part, are under 12 net carbs per serving. The carbs you will consume on this diet are from foods that are low on the glycemic index, such as:

- **Dark leafy greens:** spinach, bok choy, chard

- **Cruciferous vegetables:** cabbage, kale, radishes, cauliflower

- **Other above-ground vegetables:** celery, zucchini, summer squash

- **High-fat dairy:** heavy (whipping) cream, half-and-half (substitute with single cream in the United Kingdom), Greek yogurt, Parmesan and Cheddar cheeses

- Leeks, onions, garlic, ginger

- Coconut milk

- Avocado (as a topping)

- **Nuts:** almond flour, peanut butter, walnuts, cashews

- Berries

KETO MYTHS

There are as many myths about keto as there are adherents to the diet. Some may see what I write below as a myth as well—but I want to share my perspective so you understand how I approached this book and my recipes.

MYTH #1: KETO AND LOW-CARB ARE ENTIRELY DIFFERENT THINGS.
I acknowledge that these two diets may be *somewhat* different—but only with respect to whether or not they specify a per-day carb cap. As mentioned previously, the keto diet generally requires you to stay at or below 20 grams of net carbs per day. Low-carb diets simply exhort you to eat fewer carbs. Often, the standard American diet (SAD) is used as a yardstick. Average consumption of carbohydrates is estimated at 300 grams daily for most Americans. As you can see, there's a lot of room between 20 grams and 300 grams to specify what

constitutes low-carb. Both keto and nonspecific low-carb diets typically emphasize consuming lower amounts of carbohydrates, similar amounts of proteins, and higher quantities of fat than are consumed in the SAD.

MYTH #2: CERTAIN INGREDIENTS ARE SIMPLY NOT "ALLOWED" ON KETO. Religion, politics, and keto diet rules—these are the known controversies we all avoid discussing with others, aren't they? Here's my approach to keto. I completely exclude excessively high glycemic index foods, such as pasta, rice, potatoes, bread, flour, and sugar. These foods are known to spike blood sugar and insulin for absolutely everyone. I advocate not eating sugar, not even in small quantities. Sugar causes a spike in insulin and often results in cravings for sugar that can derail a well-progressing keto dieter.

Other than that, I eat real food, and I watch macros carefully. So, yes, my Almond-Carrot Cake (page 144) includes carrots, and I might put two low-carb corn tortillas in a pot of Chicken Tortilla Soup (page 56). Several recipes call for the selective use of tomatoes. What matters to me is that the overall carb count remains low.

MYTH #3: EATING KETO MEANS I HAVE TO EAT ALL THE FAT GRAMS MY CALCULATOR SPECIFIES. Most experts agree that we should eat only as much fat as is needed for satiety, especially if you are trying to lose weight. Your goal is to get your body to burn stored fat. This is much harder than burning the fat you eat, which is more readily available for fuel. So your highly efficient body is going to burn the fat you eat for fuel before it starts tapping into your stored reserves. If you keep eating more fat than your body needs to burn for fuel, not only will you not lose fat, but you could gain some fat, which is not what you're going for. The main reason fat makes up such a high proportion of keto diets is because it does not raise insulin. If you're hungry, fat not only satiates quickly, but it does so without raising insulin secretion.

MYTH #4: CALORIES DON'T MATTER. Sadly, calories do still matter, for the most part. The type of calories you eat (those from carbs versus protein versus fat) matters quite a lot. It is simply not possible to lose weight while eating many more calories than your body can burn.

MYTH #5: HIGHER LEVELS OF KETOSIS FOR THE WIN! Higher levels of ketones do not cause greater fat loss. Being in ketosis is much more important than the level of that ketosis. While it's fun to pee on the keto screening strips and brag about the various colors your strips turn, recognize this for what it is—fun and games. As long as you are in ketosis, you are burning fat.

Mind the Protein

Consuming the correct amounts of fat and carbs is very important when you're following the keto diet. However, getting the third macro, protein, right is also crucial. As I said, keto is a moderate-protein diet (about 15 to 30 percent of your daily calories). You should follow your online keto calculator to determine your personal protein needs. Here are some keto-friendly, moderate-protein foods:

- Pork chop (4 ounces): 27 grams protein
- Beef steak (4 ounces): 27 grams protein
- Chicken breast (4 ounces): 26 grams protein
- Salmon (4 ounces): 23 grams protein
- Ground beef, 20 percent fat (4-ounces): 20 grams protein
- Ground lamb (4 ounces): 19 grams protein

- Chicken thigh (4 ounces): 17 grams protein
- Bacon (4 slices): 13 grams protein
- Eggs (2 large): 12 grams protein
- Nut butter (2 tablespoons): 6 grams protein
- Spinach (1 cup cooked): 6 grams protein
- Almonds (¼ cup): 6 grams protein

INSTANT POT® AND KETO

Learning how to eat keto is hard enough sometimes—but cooking for it doesn't have to be. The Instant Pot® is particularly well-suited for keto cooking, due to the emphasis on proteins and vegetables—most of which cook up well in a pressure cooker. Here are a few other reasons why I use my Instant Pot® in keto cooking.

IT IS VERSATILE. It's a rice cooker, a yogurt maker, a slow cooker, and with the release of the Ultra model, even a sous vide device. It allows you more control over cooking temperatures than a stove top pressure cooker. I also use it to make keto-friendly cakes and custards. Let me tell you, when it's summer and 100 degrees outside, you will instantly appreciate not having to turn on your oven.

IT IS FAST. An Instant Pot® makes short work of tough pork shoulders, large cuts of beef, and even brisket, especially if you cut up the meat to get more even cooking, as I often advise you to do. Think 15 to 30 minutes versus 2 to 3 hours.

IT MAKES FOOD MORE FLAVORFUL. When you cook meat with a large quantity of spices, pressure cooking helps infuse the meat with additional flavor. One of the things you realize with keto—especially when you're eating what seems to be your hundredth piece of chicken for the week—is that spices are what keep it interesting. The pressure cooker allows spice flavors to meld together quickly, and the resulting taste is like that of slow-cooked meat.

IT SAVES YOU MONEY. If you aren't very intentional, eating keto can get a little expensive. Pressure cooking does an excellent job of breaking down and tenderizing tougher cuts of meat, allowing you to purchase less expensive meat while still preparing melt-in-your-mouth weeknight dinners. It also helps melt down fattier cuts of meat for a lovely mouth feel. For leaner cuts of meat, it helps break down the connective tissue to soften the meat.

IT HELPS WITH MEAL PREP. Keto can be one of those eating plans where failing to plan is akin to planning to fail. If you wait until you're ravenous to start thinking of cooking, your blood sugar will drop, and at that point you may start thinking of falling face first into a large and sugary cake. All the meals in this cookbook—with the exception of the seafood dishes—can be made ahead and frozen. I often freeze half of everything I make in single-serving portions, which I can then reheat in 3 minutes in the microwave.

IT SIMPLIFIES CLEANUP. In keeping with my "I am lazy/I am efficient" mode, I love having only one pot to clean when I'm done cooking. I use just the Instant Pot® for the most part, except for a few recipes where caramelizing really matters, and other recipes that require me to use a pot set inside the insert.

INSTANT POT® 101

There are a couple of considerations when it comes to getting your head around the Instant Pot®: how it works and how the heck to use it. I discuss both here.

The Instant Pot® in Brief

The Instant Pot® combines several kitchen appliances in one: As I mentioned, it's a rice cooker, slow cooker, and yogurt maker. Some models can even cook sous vide. But for most users, its most popular function is as a pressure cooker.

Cooking with a pressure cooker is the only way a home cook can change the boiling point of water (without moving to a different altitude). In the sealed cooking environment of a pressure cooker, the steam generated by boiling liquid inside can't escape, so as it builds up, the boiling point is raised. In the Instant Pot®, the typical high pressure of 11.6 pounds per square inch can raise the boiling temperature to 245°F (118°C).

The higher cooking temperature not only results in a faster cooking time, but also adds flavor (as I explain in more detail on page 10), as the physical reactions that produce new flavor molecules happen faster at higher temperatures.

The Instant Pot® offers several advantages over other electric pressure cookers. Many cooks prefer the stainless inner cooking pot to the nonstick versions that are standard in most other brands (but if you like a nonstick pot for some dishes, Instant Pot® also makes inner pots with a ceramic nonstick coating). Other helpful features include a trivet with handles that make it a breeze to remove a hot pot-in-pot cooking dish, and a design that lets you rest the pot lid in a slot on the handle.

The Instant Pot® makes it easy to switch from sealing to venting—and the Ultra model seals automatically, so you don't even have to remember to check it.

Using Instant Pot® Settings

I understand. There are simply so many settings. Standing in front of your new Instant Pot®, you stare at the control panel, wondering if you're about to cook dinner or launch a rocket ship with the instrument panel that has stopped many a hungry person in her tracks.

I'm going to make this very easy for you. In this book, almost all of the recipes use just TWO settings: Sauté and Pressure Cook (for those with the Ultra model) or Manual (for those with the DUO or LUX models). That's it. Really, that's all you need to cook the vast majority of these dishes.

Having said that, I think it's good to understand what the other settings do. In this section, I describe each setting. (If you're more of a visual learner, I have a video on this topic on my blog as well.)

It is a common misperception that all the settings are really the same, just programmed with different times. That is actually not the case. Many—but not all—of the buttons are unique in some combination of time, pressure, and temperature.

According to my testing, there are six settings that have specific functions rather than just different time programs, so I focus here on those settings and what they do.

SAUTÉ. This functions exactly like a stove top to brown and sear, and you can set it to high, medium, or low temperatures. This setting does not pressure cook your food; it heats and browns it.

PRESSURE COOK/MANUAL. This will likely be your most frequently used setting. For the Ultra model, you will use the Pressure Cook setting. For all older models of the Instant Pot®, you will use the Manual setting. They perform the same job. Each defaults to high pressure, and you are able to set specific cooking times. For example, when a recipe says *set to high pressure for 5 minutes*, this is the setting you will reach for, and then you will likely use the plus/minus buttons (or the dial) to set the time to 5 minutes. If a recipe calls for low pressure, you can adjust the pressure before setting the specific pressure cooking time.

SOUP. When you use the soup setting, the pressure cooker heats up very slowly at first, before hitting higher temperatures. It was originally designed to create non-cloudy broths for soups. I find it quite useful when you are trying to keep yogurt or other liquids from separating.

STEAM. Confusingly, it's called Steam—but it's under pressure. In other words, you're not steaming your food the same way that you would on a stove top or in a microwave. Your food is being pressure cooked. When you use this setting, the pot raises its temperature very quickly—and it stays hot. This allows the food to cook very quickly, without a longer lead time before the pot comes to pressure—useful when you're cooking delicate items such as fish or vegetables. Keep in mind that you cannot use this setting for foods that are placed directly in the inner cooking pot, as they will scorch. *You must use a trivet if you use the steam function*.

YOGURT. Oh, how many social media posts have many of us seen about yogurt in the Instant Pot®! It is often difficult to fit anything but Greek yogurt into a ketogenic diet, but making it at home ensures that you know exactly what went into it. You can also make yogurt using heavy whipping cream with a little milk mixed in. It's more like fermented cream—but it is so delicious that you won't care what it's called.

SLOW COOK. There are a lot of discussions as to whether or not an Instant Pot® can slow cook as well as a slow cooker does. My personal experience suggests that it can—with one caveat. Forget everything you know about settings on a slow cooker, because the Instant Pot® has settings of its own.

Rethinking the "Instant" in Instant Pot®

I have made every attempt to list reasonable prep times and cooking times for the recipes in this book, but know as well that the total time for a recipe also includes the time it takes for your pot to come to pressure, as well as release pressure. How long it takes for the pot to come to pressure is controlled by how full your pot is and how many servings you're making. Even if a recipe says it cooks in 15 minutes under pressure, you will want to allow yourself 30 to 45 minutes for the entire process the first time you make it.

Which brings us to the notion of "Instant." Certainly, some things cook faster in the Instant Pot® than they do by other cooking methods. Big cuts of red meats are classic examples of foods that cook in less than half the time they do on the stove. But this is not true of more delicate foods such as fish, vegetables, and some cuts of chicken, all of which you're likely to consume on the keto diet. These foods may take as long to cook in the pressure cooker as they do on the stove top. So why use the Instant Pot®? I find the Instant Pot® useful even in those circumstances for five main reasons:

No need to sauté for browning. One of the most common mistakes people make when pressure cooking is that they use the Sauté setting excessively to brown before cooking.

- Stop sautéing your meats ahead of time and just let the pressure cooker do the work of creating a web of flavors for you.

- Stop evaporating the flavorful liquids out of the meats and vegetables, and then adding plain water to compensate.

- Just cook as the recipes instruct, and you too can save time and effort while leveraging the pressure cooker's abilities.

Hands-off cooking. There is no need to watch easily overcooked foods like fish and test them repeatedly, and no need to stir constantly to keep the food from burning.

Better flavor. Cooking under pressure infuses the food with flavor in a way stove top cooking can't match. When I try the same recipe on the stove top and in an Instant Pot®, the difference is remarkable. Remember, your meat is not boiled under pressure, it's superheated. This results in a very different taste profile.

Heat efficiency. Not leaving your oven on for hours, not heating up your house, and not having smells permeate your house can be a wonderful thing. I love being able to steam fish like I did for the Chinese-Style Steamed Ginger Scallion Fish (page 68) and not have the house smell of fish for days. Not having to turn on your oven to make Keto Cheesecake (page 132) is also a wonderful thing.

Cooking on the road, in dorms, or in apartments. Many people use their Instant Pot® while traveling, camping in RVs, staying in hotel rooms, and living in dorms, where there might not be access to multiple appliances, ovens, or much counter space. The appliance's ability to multitask is a huge advantage.

So, while it might not *always* be faster than using the stove, the Instant Pot® has other advantages in terms of flavor and efficiency.

- Low on an Instant Pot® equals Keep Warm on a regular slow cooker.

- Medium on an Instant Pot® equals Low on a regular slow cooker.

- High on an Instant Pot® equals High on a regular slow cooker.

If this confusing, just remember: Don't use the Low setting to cook. Use either Medium or High, and you will be just fine.

COOKING FROM FROZEN

While it's possible to cook frozen meat in the Instant Pot®, doing so can change the texture of the meat, making it spongy in some cases and dry in others. For best results, cook frozen meats in sauce and plan to shred or chop the meat before eating, which will minimize any flaws in the texture.

It seems obvious, but it's easy to forget that you won't be able to cut frozen meat, so make sure that it's the size you want it before freezing. If you want meat for stew, cut it into cubes. If you have a roast, be sure that it will fit in the Instant Pot® before freezing. Also note that meat that is frozen in a flat layer—chicken thighs frozen in a single layer in a zip-top bag for example—is much easier to cook evenly than a big hunk o' chicken in a lump.

If meat is packaged in foam trays, it can be difficult to remove the moisture pad after freezing, so it's best to repackage meat before freezing. And before freezing a whole chicken, make sure to remove the bag of gizzards if one is inside.

ESSENTIAL INGREDIENTS

When I say essential ingredients, I mean it. With the exception of just a handful of ingredients, everything in this cookbook can be found in any non-keto household. Personally, I don't want to buy six kinds of weird flours and four different kinds of sweeteners, and I assume you don't either! This kind of hassle undoes all the ease of using the Instant Pot®, not to mention adding unnecessary expense (and possibly chemicals) to our meals.

Here are the *everyday* pantry and refrigerator staple ingredients used most frequently in this book:

- Cayenne
- Chiles, mild green such as poblanos
- Coconut milk, full-fat canned
- Cumin, ground
- Garam masala
- Garlic
- Ginger
- Onions
- Paprika
- Spice mix ingredients (cumin seeds, coriander seeds, whole cloves, cardamom seeds, dried red chiles, bay leaves, cinnamon sticks, dried oregano, ground cinnamon, allspice, ground coriander)
- Tomatoes, canned
- Tomatoes with chiles, canned (Ro-Tel brand)
- Turmeric, ground

As you'll see, I use only one type of flour: almond flour. That's because I prefer to simplify my pantry with one all-purpose flour rather than have four different kinds of flours and use about 2 tablespoons of each before they go back into the pantry. Almond flour is nutritious and low-carb, and it bakes well. Please do not be surprised if you swap the almond flour for coconut flour and your recipe fails. Coconut flour absorbs water like a sponge and produces much drier baked goods. You usually have to add additional eggs and additional liquids to make coconut flour recipes work.

I also use a few ingredients that may be considered out of the ordinary for the standard American diet, but which are essential for keto:

- Xanthan gum
- Swerve®
- Truvia®

Note that Swerve and Truvia can be used interchangeably in making the recipes in this cookbook.

Finally, I love to use ingredients from a variety of cuisines. This is not a keto cookbook of adapted American favorites. In these pages, you'll find my versions of recipes inspired by Chinese, Indian, Korean, and Thai cuisines, to name a few. Here is a brief intro to the ingredients that will help you pull them off:

GOCHUJANG. Used in Korean cooking, this is a fermented chile paste that has no substitute. Although it is called a chile paste and it looks a dauntingly spicy red, this is not a blisteringly hot chile paste. Rather, it contains a great complement of spicy, sweet, garlicky, and umami flavors that is unparalleled. You can use it in the recipes when called for, but here are some other ways to get the most out of *gochujang*:

- Mix it with tomato sauces and soups for an earthy, robust flavor.

- Mix it with mayonnaise for a dip that's to die for.

- Mix it with cream cheese and use as a dip.

- Add a little to a brothy soup that's falling flat.

DOUBANJIANG. A critical staple in Chinese Sichuan cuisine, this spicy, salty, fermented bean paste is yet another way to add zip and zing to your daily dishes. Often used as a simple dressing for zoodles (zucchini noodles), it is also a staple ingredient in *ma-po* tofu and many cold salads. It is similar to Korean *doenjang*. Get the Pixian type of *doubanjiang* if you can, as it contains more of the traditional, fermented ingredients and therefore more flavor.

THAI CURRY PASTE. I'm a big fan of making spices and flavor pastes from scratch, but even I use prepared Thai curry pastes, as do many accomplished Thai cooks. A good curry paste requires little bits of so many different ingredients that acquiring all the ingredients for it can be as much if not more of a challenge than actually making it. Moreover, since the commercially prepared ones are often so well made, I'd rather use the time I save by buying them to cook—or eat!—more Thai curry. For these recipes, you can use green, yellow, or red curry pastes to get different taste profiles from a single soup or curry recipe.

INSTANT POT® TROUBLESHOOTING

Instant Pot® failures happen. Here are some common ones, along with reasons why they happen and (where applicable) what you can do about them.

MY FOOD BURNED. These recipes have been well tested. If you followed them but still ended up with burned food, there are a few possible reasons why this happened:

- Your seal wasn't on correctly, and all the water evaporated.

- Your lid wasn't on correctly, and all the water evaporated.

- You forgot to move the valve from venting to sealing, and all the water evaporated.

- You had less water than the recipe called for.

- You substituted ingredients that release less water than the ingredients the recipe calls for do.

- You didn't sufficiently deglaze the pot before pressure cooking. One of the built-in safety features is that the Instant Pot® doesn't come to pressure if something is stuck or burned to the bottom.

MY POT IS SPITTING STEAM! HELP! It is not unusual for the pot to release a little steam until it comes up to pressure. Once the valve floats up and seals, it should stop leaking steam. If you're getting a steady flow of steam, however, the seal is not on tightly or needs replacing.

MY LID WON'T OPEN. If your lid won't open, the pot is likely under pressure. Do *not* force it! Wait for all the pressure to be released before you try again. Forcing it can result in serious burns and injuries. If you've been waiting for 25 to 30 minutes and it still won't open and the float valve is still up, it is possible something is stuck under the valve. Very carefully, using a long-handled spoon or fork, tap gently on the float valve. This is usually enough to get the valve to drop. Clean the lid and the valve carefully before you begin the next cooking cycle.

MY LID WON'T CLOSE. If your lid won't close, the most likely culprit is the sealing ring. Remove it and reinsert it, following the directions that came with the Instant Pot®. Ensure there is no food or debris lodged into the sides of the lid or the rim of the pot. Ensure that the liner you're using is the correct one. I have several different sizes of Instant Pot®, and I've tried to use a 5-quart liner in a 6-quart pot. Luckily for your safety, the pot won't lock or come to pressure if you try this.

The second most common reason is that you've opened the pot up, decided you needed to cook the food a little more, and now the lid won't go back on easily. The steam in the pot often pushes the valve up in these situations. What works for me is to turn the float valve to venting to allow some of that steam to dissipate, and to try again.

I'VE BEEN WAITING FOREVER FOR THE PIN TO DROP, BUT IT SAYS IT'S STILL LOCKED. Define forever 😊. Okay, wisecracks aside, realize that a very full pot takes longer to come to pressure and longer to release pressure. A pot filled with liquids is especially susceptible to this, taking longer for both come to pressure and to release pressure. If you are sure you've given it plenty of time on its own, it is likely that your float valve is stuck. Very carefully, using a long-handled spoon or fork, tap gently on the float valve. This is usually enough to get the valve to drop. Clean the lid and the valve carefully before the next cooking cycle.

THIS BOOK'S RECIPES

All right, my fellow keto-ers and low-carbers! We're about to get cooking. First, a few tips for cooking these recipes with your Instant Pot®.

I tested (and retested!) all the Instant Pot® recipes in either a 6-quart Duo, a 6-quart Ultra, or a 3-quart Mini. Each model has its own nuances, so I've tried to keep the instructions as generic as possible.

Time is always a factor when you decide to use your Instant Pot®. The recipes using the Instant Pot® break down for you the time required for every step (prep, sauté, pressure cook, pressure release), which the total time takes into consideration.

Keep these time-related particularities in mind:

- All my recipes assume that it takes about 10 minutes for the pot to come to pressure. The total times given in the recipes that use the pressure cooker factor in 10 minutes for coming to pressure.

- Many recipes call for releasing pressure naturally, which tends to take anywhere from 10 to 15 minutes. The total times given in recipes that call for natural release allow 15 minutes for the pressure release.

- Several recipes call for releasing pressure quickly, which typically takes 1 minute or less. The total times given in recipes that call for quick release do not factor in any time for the pressure release.

While these recipes could not be more hands-off, you must factor in some time beyond the time it takes to cook at pressure. The majority of the recipes can be made, start to finish, in 45 minutes or less. A number of others take 60 minutes or less.

Wherever there is a dairy-free, gluten-free, soy-free, vegan, or vegetarian recipe in the book, you'll see a label so you know that. And I think we can all agree that some of our favorite recipes to make (if not to eat) require little more than adding the ingredients to the pot, starting cooking, and walking away. I call these "pour and cook" recipes. Each of these recipes is labeled "pour and cook" so you know your effort will be truly minimal.

This cookbook emphasizes very low-carb food with an international flair that is fast and easy to make, authentic to its origins, and varied in its options. Here are my final tips:

FOCUS ON WHAT YOU CAN HAVE. Many people on keto focus on what they can't have. I prefer to focus on the things I can have, because it's hard to complain about a way of eating that allows you to eat butter, cream, cheese, lobster, steak, most vegetables, and avocados! This cookbook includes a variety of ingredients to keep your tastebuds satisfied.

EAT THE WORLD. There are only so many ways you can eat chicken before you're sick of it—or are there? What if you make Chicken Tortilla Soup (page 56) one day, Now and Later Butter Chicken (page 82) the next day, Thai Green Curry (page 89) after that, Chicken Shawarma (page 94) the next, and finish up with

West African Peanut Stew (page 80)? A whole world of food awaits you, and this cookbook gives you recipes from across the globe that are easy, authentic, and low-carb.

LEVERAGE THE POWER OF THE INSTANT POT®. When I buy an Instant Pot® cookbook that requires me to sauté on the stove top, bake in the oven, fry in an air fryer, cook in the Instant Pot®—all for one dish sometimes—I am driven mad. Very few dishes in this cookbook require this type of Mad Chef cooking. Most cook with just the Instant Pot®, with some recipes suggesting different ways you can finish them off if you so choose.

ENJOY THESE RECIPES WITH 12 GRAMS OR LESS OF NET CARBS. The cookbook includes recipes that are 12 grams or less of net carbs per serving. Although I've made every effort to provide correct nutritional information for the recipes, your specific ingredients will matter. I urge you to use a reliable resource to calculate net carbs when you make your own customizations.

CONSIDER SERVING SIZES. The recipes count 4 ounces of meat as a serving, as the USDA recommends. If other ingredients such as vegetables are added, they count 3 ounces of meat and the other ingredients as a serving. If you eat the whole pot of soup, your tummy may be happy, but your carb counts may be off.

YOU'RE NOW READY TO START COOKING. Get out your spices and your Instant Pot®, eat well, and keep calm and keto on!

2

Eggs and Vegetables

Broccoli, Ham, and Pepper Frittata, page 20

Broccoli, Ham, and Pepper Frittata

SERVES 4

This tasty frittata cooks up light and fluffy in your Instant Pot® and makes a great low-carb, keto dish that's perfect for breakfast or brunch. It's as pretty on the underside with its layer of ham and peppers as it is on the top. Either way, it's delicious and filling.

Vegetable oil or unsalted butter, for greasing the pan

1 cup sliced bell peppers

8 ounces ham, cubed

2 cups frozen broccoli florets

4 eggs

1 cup half-and-half

1 teaspoon salt

2 teaspoons freshly ground black pepper

1 cup grated Cheddar cheese

PREP TIME
10 minutes

PRESSURE COOK/MANUAL
20 minutes high pressure

RELEASE
Natural 10 minutes, then Quick

TOTAL TIME
50 minutes

MACROS
60% Fat
9% Carbs
31% Protein

GLUTEN-FREE

SOY-FREE

1. Grease a 6-by-3-inch pan extremely well so the egg does not stick to it once cooked. I use a silicone brush to get oil or butter into every crevice of the pan.

2. Arrange the sliced peppers in the bottom of the pan. Place the cubed ham on top. Cover with the frozen broccoli.

3. In a medium bowl, whisk together the eggs, half-and-half, salt, and pepper. Stir in the cheese.

4. Pour the egg mixture over the vegetables and ham. Cover the pan with aluminum foil or a silicone lid.

5. Pour 2 cups of water into the inner cooking pot of the Instant Pot®, then place a trivet in the pot. Place the covered pan on the trivet.

6. Lock the lid into place. Select Manual or Pressure Cook and adjust the pressure to High. Cook for 20 minutes. When the cooking is complete, let the pressure release naturally for 10 minutes, then quick-release any remaining pressure. Unlock the lid.

7. Carefully remove the pan from the pot and remove the foil. Let the frittata sit for 5 to 10 minutes. Using a knife, gently loosen the sides of the frittata. Place a plate on top of the pan and, holding it in place, invert the frittata onto the plate. If you want the pepper and ham side up, you're done. If you want the cheese side up, flip it on a plate once more.

8. Serve as is, or brown the top of the frittata under the broiler for 3 to 4 minutes.

Per Serving Calories: 396; Total Fat: 27g; Total Carbs: 9g; Net Carbs: 6g; Fiber: 3g; Sugar: 3g; Protein: 30g

On-the-Go Egg Cups

SERVES 4

Individual egg cups allow you to customize each one for a variety of flavors, which makes them perfect for picky families or variety junkies. For this recipe, you'll need four half-pint, wide-mouth heatproof glass jars, which will go right into the Instant Pot®. I usually make these for the week and reheat them in the microwave for 30 seconds. Do yourself a favor—grease the jars well. Otherwise, the egg sticks to the jar, and you'll drive yourself mad getting them out.

Unsalted butter or vegetable oil, for greasing the jars

4 eggs

1 cup diced vegetables, such as onions, bell peppers, mushrooms, or tomatoes

½ cup grated sharp Cheddar cheese

¼ cup half-and-half

1 teaspoon salt

1 teaspoon freshly ground black pepper

2 tablespoons chopped fresh cilantro or other herb of choice (optional)

½ cup shredded cheese of choice, for garnish

PREP TIME
10 minutes

PRESSURE COOK/MANUAL
5 minutes high pressure

RELEASE
Quick

TOTAL TIME
25 minutes

MACROS
62% Fat
12% Carbs
26% Protein

GLUTEN-FREE

SOY-FREE

VEGETARIAN

UNDER 45 MINUTES

1. Grease the inside of each jar with butter or oil. I use a silicone brush to get it into every crevice.

2. In a medium bowl, beat the eggs and stir in the vegetables, cheese, half-and-half, salt, pepper, and cilantro (if using). Divide the mixture among four half-pint wide-mouth, heatproof glass jars or other heatproof containers. Place the lids on top of the jars, but do not tighten. (The lids keep water out of the eggs.)

3. Pour 2 cups of water into the inner cooking pot of the Instant Pot®, then place a trivet in the pot. Place the egg jars on the trivet.

4. Lock the lid into place. Select Manual or Pressure Cook and adjust the pressure to High. Cook for 5 minutes. When the cooking is complete, quick-release the pressure.

5. Remove the lids from the jars and top each egg with the cheese of your choice.

6. Place the eggs under the broiler or in an air fryer for 2 to 3 minutes, until the cheese on top is melted and lightly browned.

Per Serving Calories: 239; Total Fat: 17g; Total Carbs: 7g; Net Carbs: 5g; Fiber: 2g; Sugar: 2g; Protein: 15g

Poblano and Cheese Frittata

SERVES 4

One taste of this frittata, and you'll see why it is one of my most popular recipes. If you can't find the canned chiles (which should be poblano chiles) in your neck of the woods, use fresh poblanos or other mild peppers. Make sure to soften the fresh peppers in the microwave for 2 minutes before combining them with the other ingredients.

Vegetable oil or unsalted butter, for greasing the pan

4 eggs

1 cup half-and-half

1 (10-ounce) can chopped green chiles, drained

1½ teaspoons salt

½ teaspoon ground cumin

1 cup Mexican blend shredded cheese, divided (see Tip)

¼ cup chopped fresh cilantro

1. Grease a 6-by-3-inch pan extremely well with the oil or butter.

2. In a medium bowl, beat the eggs and stir in the half-and-half, chiles, salt, cumin, and ½ cup of cheese. Pour the mixture into the prepared pan and cover with aluminum foil.

3. Pour 2 cups of water into the inner cooking pot of the Instant Pot®, then place a trivet in the pot. Place the pan on the trivet.

4. Lock the lid into place. Select Manual or Pressure Cook and adjust the pressure to High. Cook for 20 minutes. When the cooking is complete, let the pressure release naturally for 10 minutes, then quick-release any remaining pressure. Unlock the lid.

PREP TIME
10 minutes

PRESSURE COOK/MANUAL
20 minutes high pressure

RELEASE
Natural 10 minutes, then Quick

TOTAL TIME
50 minutes

MACROS
69% Fat
8% Carbs
23% Protein

GLUTEN-FREE

SOY-FREE

VEGETARIAN

TIP: *Mexican blend shredded cheese is commonly found in American grocery stores. For those unfamilar, it is a blend of Cheddar, Colby, and Monterey Jack cheeses, in equal amounts.*

5. Carefully remove the pan from the Instant Pot® and remove the foil. Scatter the remaining ½ cup of cheese on top of the frittata. Place it under a hot broiler for 2 to 5 minutes, or until cheese is bubbling and brown.

6. Let the frittata sit for 5 to 10 minutes. Using a knife, gently loosen the sides from the pan. Place a plate on top of the pan and, holding it in place, invert the frittata onto the plate. If you want the cheese and chiles side up, flip it on a plate once more.

Per Serving Calories: 283; Total Fat: 22g; Total Carbs: 7g; Net Carbs: 6g; Fiber: 1g; Sugar: 1g; Protein: 16g

Egg Loaf

SERVES 6

An egg loaf is a quick way to make eggs for sides or for quick bites like egg salad or chopped hard-boiled eggs with salt and pepper. No peeling required! But, yes, you will wonder at that alien-looking creation that pops out of your Instant Pot®. Trust me, it's worth it to make eggs like this.

Unsalted butter, for greasing the bowl

6 eggs

2 cups water, for steaming

1. Grease a heatproof bowl with the butter extremely well.

2. Crack the eggs into the greased bowl, keeping the yolks intact. Cover the bowl with aluminum foil, and set aside briefly.

3. Pour the water into the inner cooking pot of the Instant Pot® and place a trivet on top.

4. Place the foil-covered bowl of eggs on the trivet.

5. Lock the lid into place. Select Manual or Pressure Cook and adjust the pressure to High. Cook for 4 minutes. When the cooking is complete, quick-release the pressure.

6. Carefully remove the bowl from the pot. Pop out the egg loaf from the bowl. You'll see mainly a loaf of egg white, with just a few spots of egg yolk.

PREP TIME
5 minutes

PRESSURE COOK/MANUAL
4 minutes high pressure

RELEASE
Quick

TOTAL TIME
20 minutes

MACROS
64% Fat
2% Carbs
34% Protein

GLUTEN-FREE

SOY-FREE

VEGETARIAN

5 INGREDIENTS OR LESS

POUR AND COOK

UNDER 45 MINUTES

7. Chop the egg loaf as coarse or fine as you'd like. You can now mix it with a little mayonnaise for egg salad, stir it with a little butter, salt, and pepper for a quick snack or meal, or use it for whatever you'd like.

Per Serving Calories: 74; Total Fat: 5g; Total Carbs: 0g; Net Carbs: 0g; Fiber: 0g; Sugar: 0g; Protein: 6g

Cauliflower Mac and Cheese

SERVES 4

This recipe receives universal raves, and with good reason—it's creamy, it's rich, it's easy to make, and it's keto. What's not to love? This might just be the recipe to convert those self-proclaimed haters of cauliflower.

2 cups Cauliflower Rice (page 149)

2 tablespoons cream cheese, at room temperature

½ cup half-and-half

½ cup grated sharp Cheddar cheese

1 teaspoon salt

1 teaspoon freshly ground black pepper

1. In a heatproof bowl, mix the cauliflower, cream cheese, half-and-half, Cheddar cheese, salt, and pepper together. Cover the bowl with aluminum foil.

2. Pour 2 cups of water into the inner cooking pot of the Instant Pot®, then place a trivet in the pot. Place the bowl on the trivet.

3. Lock the lid into place. Select Manual or Pressure Cook and adjust the pressure to High. Cook for 5 minutes. When the cooking is complete, let the pressure release naturally for 10 minutes, then quick-release any remaining pressure. Unlock the lid and carefully remove the bowl. Remove the foil.

4. Place the cooked cauliflower under the broiler, and broil until the cheese is brown and bubbling, 3 to 5 minutes. Serve immediately.

PREP TIME
5 minutes

PRESSURE COOK/MANUAL
5 minutes high pressure

RELEASE
Natural 10 minutes, then Quick

TOTAL TIME
30 minutes

MACROS
70% Fat
13% Carbs
17% Protein

GLUTEN-FREE

SOY-FREE

VEGETARIAN

5 INGREDIENTS OR LESS

UNDER 45 MINUTES

Per Serving Calories: 134; Total Fat: 11g; Total Carbs: 4g; Net Carbs: 3g; Fiber: 1g; Sugar: 2g; Protein: 6g

Mexican-Style Zucchini and Poblanos

SERVES 6

This recipe comes together quickly, and allows you to buy a few poblanos in a given week and make two or three different things out of the same ingredient. I used ground pork to add a little body to this dish, but you can substitute it with the ground meat of your choice.

1 tablespoon vegetable oil

2 poblano peppers, seeded and cut lengthwise into ½-inch strips

2 teaspoons unsalted butter

½ onion, thinly sliced

1 tablespoon minced garlic

1 pound ground pork

1 zucchini, cut into thick rounds

1 yellow crookneck squash, cut into thick rounds

½ cup chicken broth

½ teaspoon ground cumin

1 teaspoon salt

1 tablespoon Mexican crema or sour cream

PREP TIME
5 minutes

SAUTÉ
10 minutes

PRESSURE COOK/MANUAL
2 minutes low pressure

RELEASE
Quick

TOTAL TIME
30 minutes

MACROS
73% Fat
4% Carbs
23% Protein

GLUTEN-FREE

SOY-FREE

UNDER 45 MINUTES

1. Preheat the Instant Pot® by selecting Sauté and adjusting to high heat. When the inner cooking pot is hot, add the oil and heat until it is shimmering. Add the poblano strips in a single layer, working in batches if necessary, and char on both sides, flipping only occasionally, for about 10 minutes.

2. Add the butter to the pot. Once melted, add the onion and garlic, and sauté until soft, 2 to 3 minutes.

3. Add the ground pork and break it up in chunks, mixing it well with the vegetables. Cook until the lumps are broken up in the meat, and it is half-way cooked, about 4 to 5 minutes.

4. Add the zucchini, squash, broth, cumin, and salt to the pot.

5. Lock the lid into place. Select Manual or Pressure Cook and adjust the pressure to Low. Cook for 2 minutes. When the cooking is complete, quick-release the pressure. Unlock the lid.

6. Stir in the crema so it incorporates into the sauce.

Per Serving Calories: 248; Total Fat: 20g; Total Carbs: 3g; Net Carbs: 2g; Fiber: 1g; Sugar: 1g; Protein: 14g

Baba Ghanoush

MAKES ABOUT 1½ CUPS

The trick to making this Middle Eastern eggplant dip is to char the eggplant well. Doing so gives the dip the slightly smoky flavor that is its hallmark, along with the liquid smoke you're going to add. The lemon juice, parsley, oil, and paprika added at the end lend a lovely freshness to the cooked dish.

6 tablespoons vegetable oil, divided

1 eggplant, peeled, halved crosswise, then sliced lengthwise into ½-inch-thick planks

5 garlic cloves, minced

½ teaspoon salt

¼ cup water

2 tablespoons tahini

1 to 2 tablespoons freshly squeezed lemon juice

¼ teaspoon liquid smoke

2 tablespoons chopped parsley

1 tablespoon extra-virgin olive oil

Pinch smoked paprika

PREP TIME
10 minutes

SAUTÉ
15 minutes

PRESSURE COOK/MANUAL
3 minutes high pressure

RELEASE
Quick

TOTAL TIME
40 minutes

MACROS
85% Fat
12% Carbs
3% Protein

DAIRY-FREE

GLUTEN-FREE

SOY-FREE

VEGAN

UNDER 45 MINUTES

1. Preheat the Instant Pot® by selecting Sauté and adjusting to high heat. When the inner cooking pot is hot, add 2 tablespoons of oil and heat until it is shimmering.

2. Add one layer of eggplant slices. Do not stir or disturb them until they are properly charred on the bottom. Without this char, you won't get the smoky taste you need. Once these slices char, they will shrink a bit and you can move them to the side of the pot and add more eggplant slices. With each new round of eggplant slices, you will need to add more oil to the pot. Charring all the eggplant slices will take 10 to 15 minutes. Once all the eggplant is charred, use a spatula or spoon and scrape up the char from the bottom of the pot.

3. Add the garlic, salt, and water to the pot with the charred eggplant slices.

4. Lock the lid into place. Select Manual or Pressure Cook and adjust the pressure to High. Cook for 3 minutes. When the cooking is complete, quick-release the pressure. Unlock the lid.

5. If there is too much water in the bottom when you remove the lid, turn the Instant Pot® to Sauté and let some of it cook off.

6. Tilt the pot slightly. Using an immersion blender, roughly purée the eggplant mixture. Unless you are feeding it to a baby, do not purée until smooth.

7. Stir in the tahini, lemon juice, and liquid smoke. Taste and adjust the seasoning as needed.

8. Spoon into a bowl, top with the parsley and olive oil, and sprinkle with the smoked paprika.

9. Serve with raw veggies, such as green beans or celery.

Per Serving (2 tablespoons) Calories: 96; Total Fat: 9g; Total Carbs: 3g; Net Carbs: 1g; Fiber: 2g; Sugar: 1g; Protein: 1g

Green Beans with Bacon

SERVES 6

If someone asks me if these green beans are "squeakers," I know I'm with a true Southerner. They're not squeakers, and they're not mush. They're kind of a wonderful in-between of tender, well-cooked beans with a little texture. Just beans, bacon, onion and seasonings make this a fast and easy dish in your Instant Pot®.

6 slices bacon, diced

1 cup diced onion

4 cups halved green beans

¼ cup water

1 teaspoon salt, plus more for seasoning

1 teaspoon freshly ground black pepper, plus more for seasoning

1. Preheat the Instant Pot® by selecting Sauté and adjusting to high heat. Add the bacon and onion and sauté for 2 to 3 minutes.

2. Add the green beans, water, salt, and pepper to the pot.

3. Lock the lid into place. Select Manual or Pressure Cook and adjust the pressure to High. Cook for 4 minutes. When the cooking is complete, quick-release the pressure. Unlock the lid.

4. Taste and season with additional salt and pepper if needed before serving.

Per Serving Calories: 165; Total Fat: 13g; Total Carbs: 6g; Net Carbs: 3g; Fiber: 3g; Sugar: 2g; Protein: 6g

PREP TIME
10 minutes

SAUTÉ
5 minutes

PRESSURE COOK/MANUAL
4 minutes high pressure

RELEASE
Quick

TOTAL TIME
30 minutes

MACROS
71% Fat
15% Carbs
14% Protein

DAIRY-FREE

GLUTEN-FREE

SOY-FREE

5 INGREDIENTS OR LESS

UNDER 45 MINUTES

Quick Indian Creamy Eggplant

SERVES 6

If this eggplant dish is new to you, it's for good reason—because I made it up! But you also won't be able to stop eating it—that spicy, creamy goodness is just going to make you want more and more of this. Thankfully, it's easy to prep and easy to pressure cook.

½ teaspoon peanut oil

1 small onion, thinly sliced

1 tomato, chopped

4 cups chopped eggplant

¼ teaspoon ground turmeric

¼ teaspoon cayenne

¼ teaspoon Garam Masala (page 151)

¼ teaspoon amchoor or chaat masala (optional)

¼ teaspoon goda masala or chana masala (optional)

¼ teaspoon salt

¼ cup heavy (whipping) cream

PREP TIME
15 minutes

PRESSURE COOK/MANUAL
4 minutes low pressure

RELEASE
Natural 10 minutes, then Quick

SAUTÉ
2 minutes

TOTAL TIME
40 minutes

MACROS
62% Fat
33% Carbs
5% Protein

GLUTEN-FREE

SOY-FREE

VEGETARIAN

UNDER 45 MINUTES

1. Add the oil to the inner cooking pot of the Instant Pot®. Place the onion, tomato, and eggplant on top, in that order. You want the onion and tomato at the bottom to help create the moisture needed for this dish to cook, since you aren't adding any additional water.

2. Over the top of the vegetables, sprinkle the turmeric, cayenne, garam masala, amchoor (if using), goda masala (if using), and salt. Do not stir.

3. Lock the lid on the Instant Pot®. Select Manual and adjust to Low pressure. Cook for 4 minutes.

4. When the cooking is complete, allow the pressure to release naturally for 10 minutes, then quick-release any remaining pressure.

5. Select Sauté and adjust to More for high heat. When the mixture starts to bubble, add the cream, stirring well to incorporate. Allow the cream to thicken a little, about 2 minutes, then serve.

Per Serving Calories: 73; Total Fat: 5g; Total Carbs: 6g; Net Carbs: 3g; Fiber: 3g; Sugar: 2g; Protein: 1g

Palak Paneer

SERVES 6

If you always wanted to prepare Indian dishes but were intimidated by the long list of ingredients, here's the recipe that will convince you otherwise. You're probably familiar with all the ingredients, and most you probably already have on hand. Better yet, it's delicious, nutritious, flavorful, and super easy to make.

2 teaspoons vegetable oil

5 garlic cloves, chopped

1 tablespoon chopped fresh ginger

½ serrano or jalapeño chile, chopped

1 large yellow onion, chopped

1 pound fresh spinach

2 tomatoes, chopped

2 teaspoons ground cumin

½ teaspoon cayenne (adjust to your preferred heat level)

2 teaspoons Garam Masala (page 151)

1 teaspoon ground turmeric

1 teaspoon salt

½ cup water

1½ cups paneer cubes

½ cup heavy (whipping) cream

PREP TIME
10 minutes

SAUTÉ
3 minutes

PRESSURE COOK/MANUAL
4 minutes high pressure

RELEASE
Natural 5 minutes, then Quick

TOTAL TIME
30 minutes

MACROS
68% Fat
17% Carbs
15% Protein

GLUTEN-FREE

SOY-FREE

VEGETARIAN

UNDER 45 MINUTES

1. Preheat the Instant Pot® by selecting Sauté and adjusting to high heat. When the inner cooking pot is hot, add the oil and heat until it is shimmering. Add the garlic, ginger, and chile, and sauté for 2 to 3 minutes.

2. Add the onion, spinach, tomatoes, cumin, cayenne, garam masala, turmeric, salt, and water.

3. Lock the lid into place. Select Manual or Pressure Cook and adjust the pressure to High. Cook for 4 minutes. When the cooking is complete, let the pressure release naturally for 5 minutes, then quick-release any remaining pressure. Unlock the lid.

4. Tilting the pot, use an immersion blender to purée the mixture. Depending on your preference, you can leave the mixture slightly chunky or purée until very smooth.

5. Gently stir in the paneer and top each serving with a drizzle of cream.

Per Serving Calories: 185; Total Fat: 14g; Total Carbs: 9g; Net Carbs: 7g; Fiber: 2g; Sugar: 2g; Protein: 7g

Creamy Poblano Peppers and Sweet Corn

SERVES 6

This is my simple, one-step version of rajas con crema y elote. *It skips the traditional charring of the poblanos—yet ends up with all the flavor of a traditional preparation. You can leave out the corn to reduce the already low-carb content even further. I included just a little bit of it for its flavor and texture.*

1 tablespoon vegetable oil

2 poblano peppers, sliced lengthwise into ½-inch-thick strips

¾ red onion, thinly sliced

½ cup frozen corn

¼ cup water

1 to 2 teaspoons salt

1 teaspoon ground cumin, plus additional for garnish

½ cup heavy (whipping) cream

Juice of ½ lemon

2 tablespoons sour cream

PREP TIME
10 minutes

SAUTÉ
8 minutes

PRESSURE COOK/MANUAL
1 minute low pressure

RELEASE
Quick

TOTAL TIME
30 minutes

MACROS
80% Fat
16% Carbs
4% Protein

SOY-FREE

VEGETARIAN

UNDER 45 MINUTES

1. Preheat the Instant Pot® by selecting Sauté and adjusting to high heat. When the inner cooking pot is hot, add the oil and heat until it is shimmering. Add the poblanos, skin-side down, in a single layer and let them char a bit without disturbing them, 5 to 8 minutes.

2. Add the onion, corn, water, salt, and cumin to the pot.

3. Lock the lid into place. Select Manual or Pressure Cook and adjust the pressure to Low. Cook for 1 minute. When the cooking is complete, quick-release the pressure. Unlock the lid.

4. While the vegetables cook, in a small bowl mix together the heavy cream, lemon juice, and sour cream to make the crema. Once the vegetables are done cooking, gently stir the crema into the pot.

5. Sprinkle the finished vegetables with a little additional cumin for fragrance if desired.

Per Serving Calories: 123; Total Fat: 11g; Total Carbs: 4g; Net Carbs: 3g; Fiber: 1g; Sugar: 1g; Protein: 2g

3

Soups

Vietnamese Bo Kho, page 46

Summary Vegetable Soup

SERVES 6

This summer soup is filled to the brim with rainbow chard and yellow summer squash. Vary the vegetables as you see fit, but don't skip the finishing step with the garlic and parsley. The burst of flavor from both those ingredients gives this soup a fresh taste that is just delightful.

3 cups finely sliced leeks

6 cups chopped rainbow chard, stems and leaves

1 cup chopped celery

2 tablespoons minced garlic, divided

1 teaspoon dried oregano

1 teaspoon salt

2 teaspoons freshly ground black pepper

3 cups chicken broth, plus more as needed

2 cups sliced yellow summer squash, ½-inch slices

¼ cup chopped fresh parsley

¾ cup heavy (whipping) cream

4 to 6 tablespoons grated Parmesan cheese

PREP TIME
10 minutes

PRESSURE COOK/MANUAL
3 minutes high pressure

RELEASE
Quick

SAUTÉ
3 minutes

TOTAL TIME
30 minutes

MACROS
60% Fat
21% Carbs
19% Protein

GLUTEN-FREE

SOY-FREE

UNDER 45 MINUTES

1. Put the leeks, chard, celery, 1 tablespoon of garlic, oregano, salt, pepper, and broth into the inner cooking pot of the Instant Pot®.

2. Lock the lid into place. Select Manual or Pressure Cook and adjust the pressure to High. Cook for 3 minutes. When the cooking is complete, quick-release the pressure. Unlock the lid.

3. Add more broth if needed.

4. Turn the pot to Sauté and adjust the heat to high. Add the yellow squash, parsley, and remaining 1 tablespoon of garlic.

5. Allow the soup to cook for 2 to 3 minutes, or until the squash is softened and cooked through.

6. Stir in the cream and ladle the soup into bowls. Sprinkle with the Parmesan cheese and serve.

Per Serving Calories: 210; Total Fat: 14g; Total Carbs: 13g; Net Carbs: 10g; Fiber: 3g; Sugar: 5g; Protein: 10g

Hamburger Stew

SERVES 6

This easy Instant Pot® hamburger stew can be made with any low-carb frozen vegetables of your choice. Family-friendly pour and cook recipes like this give you lots of taste for little effort. It's actually a great choice for those "I don't know what we're having for dinner" days.

1 pound 80% lean ground beef

½ cup tomato sauce

2 tablespoons tomato paste

1 tablespoon powdered chicken broth base

2 cups frozen green beans

1 cup sliced onions

3 tablespoons apple cider vinegar

1 tablespoon soy sauce

1 teaspoon salt

2 teaspoons freshly ground black pepper

Juice of 1 lemon

PREP TIME
10 minutes

SAUTÉ
2 minutes

PRESSURE COOK/MANUAL
5 minutes high pressure

RELEASE
Natural 10 minutes, then Quick

TOTAL TIME
40 minutes

MACROS
65% Fat
12% Carbs
23% Protein

DAIRY-FREE

POUR AND COOK

UNDER 45 MINUTES

1. Preheat the Instant Pot® by selecting Sauté and adjusting to high heat. When the inner cooking pot is hot, add the ground beef. Break up any clumps and cook for 2 to 3 minutes. You do not need to brown the beef, as the Maillard reaction in the pressure cooker will take care of this for you.

2. Add the tomato sauce, tomato paste, chicken broth base, green beans, onions, vinegar, soy sauce, salt, and pepper.

3. Lock the lid into place. Select Manual or Pressure Cook and adjust the pressure to High. Cook for 5 minutes. When the cooking is complete, let the pressure release naturally for 10 minutes, then quick-release any remaining pressure. Unlock the lid.

4. Stir in the lemon juice and serve.

TIP: *You can use the frozen vegetables of your choice for this dish. Try to stay away from cruciferous vegetables such as broccoli or cauliflower that will cook down to mush, but vegetables such as Swiss chard, okra, and kale all do well in this recipe.*

Per Serving Calories: 276; Total Fat: 20g; Total Carbs: 8g; Net Carbs: 5g; Fiber: 3g; Sugar: 5g; Protein: 16g

Vietnamese Bo Kho

SERVES 6

This one-step recipe is hearty and fragrant. It is made with beef, turnips, star anise, Chinese five-spice powder, and curry powder. My whole house smells amazing when I make it! This is the one and only instance where I use store-bought curry powder instead of making my own spice blend. Since this is not an Indian dish, I'm okay with doing that.

1 onion, roughly chopped

1 pound beef chuck stew meat cubes

2 tablespoons tomato paste

2 whole star anise

1 tablespoon lemongrass paste

1 tablespoon minced fresh ginger

1 tablespoon minced garlic

1¾ cups water, divided

½ cup coconut water

1 teaspoon freshly ground black pepper

½ teaspoon Chinese five-spice powder

½ teaspoon curry powder

1 turnip, quartered

2 carrots, chopped into large, thick chunks

PREP TIME
10 minutes

PRESSURE COOK/MANUAL
15 minutes high pressure

RELEASE
Natural 10 minutes, then Quick

TOTAL TIME
45 minutes

MACROS
60% Fat
15% Carbs
25% Protein

DAIRY-FREE

GLUTEN-FREE

SOY-FREE

POUR AND COOK

1. In the inner cooking pot of the Instant Pot®, add the onion, beef, tomato paste, star anise, lemongrass paste, ginger, garlic, 1½ cups of water, coconut water, pepper, Chinese five-spice powder, and curry powder. Place a trivet on top of the meat and spices.

2. In a smaller heatproof container, place the turnip, carrots, and remaining ¼ cup of water. Place on top of the trivet.

3. Lock the lid into place. Select Manual or Pressure Cook and adjust the pressure to High. Cook for 15 minutes. When the cooking is complete, let the pressure release naturally for 10 minutes, then quick-release any remaining pressure. Unlock the lid.

4. Remove the bowl with the vegetables and the trivet. Add the vegetables and any of their liquid to the soup, first cutting them into smaller pieces, if you like.

Per Serving Calories: 221; Total Fat: 14g; Total Carbs: 9g; Net Carbs: 7g; Fiber: 2g; Sugar: 4g; Protein: 16g

Sichuan Pork Soup

SERVES 6

This flavorful, low-carb version of Sichuan pork soup substitutes bok choy for the noodles while keeping the traditional flavors of this soup. Pressure cooking makes the meat super tender. If you love Sichuan food but have never tried cooking with doubanjiang, here's your chance to get started. Its umami, slightly pungent flavor is unique and delicious.

2 tablespoons peanut oil or other cooking oil

1 tablespoon minced garlic

1 tablespoon minced fresh ginger

2 tablespoons soy sauce

2 tablespoons black vinegar (see Tip)

1 to 2 teaspoons Truvia or Swerve

2 teaspoons Sichuan peppercorns, crushed

1 to 2 teaspoons salt

½ onion, sliced

1 pound pork shoulder, cut into 2-inch chunks

2 tablespoons doubanjiang (see page 13)

3 cups water

3 to 4 cups chopped bok choy

¼ cup chopped fresh cilantro

PREP TIME
10 minutes

SAUTÉ
3 minutes

PRESSURE COOK/MANUAL
20 minutes high pressure

RELEASE
Natural 10 minutes, then Quick

TOTAL TIME
1 hour and 5 minutes

MACROS
70% Fat
8% Carbs
22% Protein

DAIRY-FREE

POUR AND COOK

1. Preheat the Instant Pot® by selecting Sauté and adjusting to high heat. When the inner cooking pot is hot, add the oil and heat until it is shimmering. Add the garlic and ginger and sauté for 1 to 2 minutes.

2. Add the soy sauce, vinegar, sweetener, peppercorns, salt, onion, pork, doubanjiang, and water. Stir well.

3. Lock the lid into place. Select Manual or Pressure Cook and adjust the pressure to High. Cook for 20 minutes. When the cooking is complete, let the pressure release naturally for 10 minutes, then quick-release any remaining pressure. Unlock the lid.

4. Open the pot and add the bok choy. Close the lid and let it cook in the residual heat for about 10 minutes, or until softened but not mushy.

5. Ladle the soup into bowls and top with the cilantro. Serve and enjoy!

Per Serving Calories: 256; Total Fat: 20g; Total Carbs: 5g; Fiber: 1g; Net Carbs: 4g; Sugar: 2g; Protein: 14g

TIP: *If you don't have (or can't find) black vinegar, you can use white vinegar and ½ teaspoon of Swerve or Truvia instead.*

Chicken Curry Soup

SERVES 6

Reproduce the flavors of your favorite chicken curry without the use of any curry powder at all. As you probably know, curry powder is not really Indian. At all. But this soup is delicious and nourishing, and quite authentic tasting—even though I totally made it up.

1 pound boneless, skinless chicken thighs

1½ cups unsweetened coconut milk

½ onion, finely diced

3 or 4 garlic cloves, crushed

1 (2-inch) piece ginger, finely chopped

1 cup sliced mushrooms, such as cremini and shiitake

4 ounces baby spinach

1 teaspoon salt

½ teaspoon ground turmeric

½ teaspoon cayenne

1 teaspoon Garam Masala (page 151)

¼ cup chopped fresh cilantro

PREP TIME
10 minutes

PRESSURE COOK/MANUAL
10 minutes high pressure

RELEASE
Natural

TOTAL TIME
45 minutes

MACROS
62% Fat
10% Carbs
28% Protein

DAIRY-FREE

GLUTEN-FREE

SOY-FREE

1. In the inner cooking pot of your Instant Pot®, add the chicken, coconut milk, onion, garlic, ginger, mushrooms, spinach, salt, turmeric, cayenne, garam masala, and cilantro.

2. Lock the lid into place. Select Manual or Pressure Cook and adjust the pressure to High. Cook for 10 minutes. When the cooking is complete, let the pressure release naturally. Unlock the lid.

3. Use tongs to transfer the chicken to a bowl. Shred the chicken, then stir it back into the soup.

4. Eat and rejoice.

Per Serving Calories: 378; Total Fat: 26g; Total Carbs: 10g; Net Carbs: 6g; Fiber: 4g; Sugar: 4g; Protein: 26g

Poblano and Chicken Soup

SERVES 8

Even if you hate cauliflower, you might like this soup just fine, with all of its flavor coming from the other ingredients. The lovely poblanos, the hint of cumin and coriander, and the cream cheese combine to make an excellent, hearty soup. Note that the quality of poblanos can have a significant impact on the spiciness of this dish. Feel free to add canned chiles or some hot sauce if you want your soup spicier.

1 cup diced onion

3 poblano peppers, chopped

5 garlic cloves

2 cups diced cauliflower

1½ pounds chicken breast, cut into large chunks

¼ cup chopped fresh cilantro

1 teaspoon ground coriander

1 teaspoon ground cumin

1 to 2 teaspoons salt

2 cups water

2 ounces cream cheese, cut into small chunks

1 cup sour cream

PREP TIME
10 minutes

PRESSURE COOK/MANUAL
15 minutes high pressure

RELEASE
Natural 10 minutes, then Quick

SAUTÉ
5 minutes

TOTAL TIME
55 minutes

MACROS
45% Fat
16% Carbs
39% Protein

GLUTEN-FREE

SOY-FREE

1. To the inner cooking pot of the Instant Pot®, add the onion, poblanos, garlic, cauliflower, chicken, cilantro, coriander, cumin, salt, and water.

2. Lock the lid into place. Select Manual or Pressure Cook and adjust the pressure to High. Cook for 15 minutes. When the cooking is complete, let the pressure release naturally for 10 minutes, then quick-release any remaining pressure. Unlock the lid.

3. Remove the chicken with tongs and place in a bowl.

4. Tilting the pot, use an immersion blender to roughly purée the vegetable mixture. It should still be slightly chunky.

5. Turn the Instant Pot® to Sauté and adjust to high heat. When the broth is hot and bubbling, add the cream cheese and stir until it melts. Use a whisk to blend in the cream cheese if needed.

6. Shred the chicken and stir it back into the pot. Once it is heated through, serve, topped with sour cream, and enjoy.

Per Serving Calories: 202; Total Fat: 10g; Total Carbs: 8g; Net Carbs: 5g; Fiber: 3g; Sugar: 3g; Protein: 20g

Hot and Sour Soup

SERVES 8

The first time I realized how many carbs are in commercial hot and sour soup, I just about fell out of my chair. Then I wanted to cry because I love hot and sour soup. It's tasty, it's spicy, it makes me feel like I'm eating something healthy—so I decided I'd make a healthy, keto-friendly version. Treat this recipe as a guide, and season to taste. Add more vinegar for tang and/or more pepper for spice, until the soup tastes right to you.

5 cups low-sodium chicken broth

1 pound boneless pork center loin chop, thinly sliced

1 cup dried woodear mushrooms (see Tip)

3 tablespoons soy sauce

1 tablespoon black vinegar or white vinegar

2 tablespoons rice vinegar or white vinegar

1 teaspoon salt

½ teaspoon xanthan gum

2 teaspoons freshly ground black pepper

3 tablespoons water

1 pound extra-firm tofu, diced

4 eggs, lightly beaten

PREP TIME
10 minutes

SOUP
10 minutes high pressure

RELEASE
Natural 10 minutes, then Quick

SAUTÉ
3 minutes

TOTAL TIME
45 minutes

MACROS
55% Fat
15% Carbs
30% Protein

DAIRY-FREE

1. In the inner cooking pot of the Instant Pot®, put the broth, pork, mushrooms, soy sauce, black vinegar, rice vinegar, salt, xanthan gum, pepper, and water.

2. Lock the lid into place. Select Soup and adjust the pressure to High. Cook for 10 minutes. When the cooking is complete, let the pressure release naturally for 10 minutes, then quick-release any remaining pressure. Unlock the lid.

3. Turn the Instant Pot® on Sauté and adjust to high heat to allow the soup to stay hot.

4. Using tongs, remove the mushrooms to a cutting board. Cut them into thin slices, then stir them back into the soup.

5. Add the tofu to the pot and stir. Slowly pour in the eggs. Mix the eggs three times around with chopsticks. Cover the pot and let the eggs cook in the broth for about 1 minute, then serve.

Per Serving Calories: 251; Total Fat: 15g; Total Carbs: 10g; Net Carbs: 10g; Fiber: 0g; Sugar: 1g; Protein: 19g

TIP: *Woodear mushrooms are the delicious slivers of black that you see in hot and sour soup. If you can't find these, substitute with any other dried mushrooms of your choice. Or if you use fresh mushrooms, add them after the soup is cooked, then press Sauté and cook for 3 to 4 minutes, until the mushrooms are heated through and softened.*

Chicken Tortilla Soup

SERVES 4

I know, I know. Can you call it chicken tortilla soup when it isn't full of tortillas? You can when it has two low-carb tortillas to thicken it up without adding much in the way of net carbs (or you can choose to omit the tortillas altogether). It tastes just like traditional chicken tortilla soup. Don't skip the step of sautéing the vegetables. The 10 minutes you spend doing that pays off in spades.

½ cup roughly chopped onion

1 cup canned diced tomatoes and their juices

2 garlic cloves

1 chipotle chile in adobo sauce from a can

1 teaspoon adobo sauce

½ jalapeño pepper

¼ cup fresh cilantro

1 to 2 teaspoons salt

1 tablespoon vegetable oil

4 cups water

2 corn tortillas, diced (optional)

2 (6-ounce) boneless, skinless chicken breasts, each cut into 4 to 6 pieces

½ cup sour cream

½ cup Mexican blend shredded cheese (see Tip on page 24)

PREP TIME
5 minutes

SAUTÉ
10 minutes

PRESSURE COOK/MANUAL
20 minutes high pressure

RELEASE
Natural 10 minutes, then Quick

TOTAL TIME
55 minutes

MACROS
60% Fat
6% Carbs
34% Protein

SOY-FREE

1. In a blender, purée the onion, tomatoes, garlic, chipotle chile, adobo sauce, jalapeño, cilantro, and salt.

2. Preheat the Instant Pot® by selecting Sauté and adjusting to high heat. When the inner cooking pot is hot, add the oil and heat until it is shimmering. Add the puréed vegetables and stir well. Cook, stirring occasionally, for about 10 minutes, or until the mixture is relatively thickened.

3. Add the water, tortillas (if using), and chicken. ➤

4. Lock the lid into place. Select Manual or Pressure Cook and adjust the pressure to High. Cook for 20 minutes. When the cooking is complete, let the pressure release naturally for 10 minutes, then quick-release any remaining pressure. Unlock the lid.

5. Use tongs to transfer the chicken to a bowl. Shred the chicken, then stir it back into the soup. Ladle the soup into bowls and serve with the sour cream and cheese.

Per Serving Calories: 256; Total Fat: 17g; Total Carbs: 4g; Net Carbs: 3g; Fiber: 1g; Sugar: 2g; Protein: 22g

Creamy Chicken and Vegetable Soup

SERVES 4

Here's a super easy, delicious, and highly customizable creamy chicken soup recipe for your Instant Pot® that you can make with whatever you have in your pantry, freezer, or refrigerator. This recipe uses a mix of frozen corn, carrots, and green beans. But almost any fresh or frozen vegetables—such as spinach, kale, chard, onions, or mushrooms—will work beautifully.

1 pound boneless, skinless chicken thighs, diced small

1 (10-ounce) bag frozen vegetables, such as a corn, carrot, and green bean mix

2 cups water

1 teaspoon poultry seasoning

1 tablespoon powdered chicken broth base

1 teaspoon salt

1 teaspoon freshly ground black pepper

1 cup heavy (whipping) cream

1. Put the chicken, vegetables, water, poultry seasoning, chicken broth base, salt, and pepper in the inner cooking pot of your Instant Pot®.

2. Lock the lid into place. Select Manual or Pressure Cook and adjust the pressure to High. Cook for 2 minutes. When the cooking is complete, quick-release the pressure (you may want to do this in short bursts so the soup doesn't spurt out). Unlock the lid.

3. Add the cream, stir, and serve. Or, if you prefer, you can mash up the chicken with the back of a wooden spoon to break it into shreds before adding the cream.

Per Serving Calories: 327; Total Fat: 19g; Total Carbs: 13g; Net Carbs: 10g; Fiber: 3g; Sugar: 5g; Protein: 26g

PREP TIME
5 minutes

PRESSURE COOK/MANUAL
2 minutes high pressure

RELEASE
Quick

TOTAL TIME
20 minutes

MACROS
53% Fat
15% Carbs
32% Protein

GLUTEN-FREE

SOY-FREE

POUR AND COOK

UNDER 45 MINUTES

TIP: *This recipe calls for raw chicken and frozen vegetables. If you opt to make the recipe instead with cooked chicken and fresh vegetables, reduce the pressure cooking time to 1 minute. Either way, when using chicken thighs, breasts, or similar cuts, it's important that the meat is diced into small pieces so it cooks in the same time as the vegetables. You can reduce carbs even more by using lower-carb veggies such as spinach, kale, Swiss chard, and green beans.*

Spicy and Creamy Chicken Soup

SERVES 4

This recipe is a classic example of why my recipes look so different from many of the others out there. Who thinks of combining tomatoes and chiles with chicken and coconut milk? No one. Well, I mean, I did. But if I can brag, this is the perfect recipe for people who like their food spiced (but not always spicy). It's bursting with flavor, and it uses ingredients found in most pantries.

1 onion, chopped

6 garlic cloves, peeled

1 (2-inch) piece fresh ginger, chopped

1 (10-ounce) can tomatoes with chiles (such as Ro-Tel, or see Tip)

1½ cups full-fat coconut milk, divided

1 tablespoon powdered chicken broth base

1 pound boneless chicken thighs, cut into large bite-size pieces

1½ cups chopped celery

2 cups chopped Swiss chard

1 teaspoon ground turmeric

1. To a blender jar, add the onion, garlic, ginger, tomatoes, ½ cup of coconut milk, and chicken broth base. Purée the ingredients into a sauce.

2. Pour the mixture into the inner cooking pot of the Instant Pot®. Add the chicken, celery, and chard.

3. Lock the lid into place. Select Manual or Pressure Cook and adjust the pressure to High. Cook for 5 minutes. When the cooking is complete, let the pressure release naturally for 10 minutes, then quick-release any remaining pressure.

4. Unlock the lid and add the remaining 1 cup of coconut milk and turmeric. Stir to heat through and serve.

Per Serving Calories: 337; Total Fat: 22g; Total Carbs: 10g; Net Carbs: 7g; Fiber: 3g; Sugar: 5g; Protein: 25g

PREP TIME
10 minutes

PRESSURE COOK/MANUAL
5 minutes high pressure

RELEASE
Natural 10 minutes, then Quick

TOTAL TIME
35 minutes

MACROS
60% Fat
11% Carbs
29% Protein

DAIRY-FREE

GLUTEN-FREE

SOY-FREE

UNDER 45 MINUTES

TIP: *If you can't find Ro-Tel brand tomatoes with chiles, substitute it with 8-ounces of canned tomatoes and 2 ounces of canned poblano chiles or other mild green chiles.*

Thai Yellow Curry Coconut Soup

SERVES 6

Curry paste, coconut milk, and fresh vegetables make for a savory, comforting twist on chicken soup. This soup is well spiced but not too spicy. It's easy to vary the spice level by adjusting how much yellow curry paste you put into it. Treat this as a base recipe and mix up the low-carb vegetables to keep it interesting.

4 boneless, skinless chicken thighs

1 (14.5-ounce) can unsweetened full-fat coconut milk

2 teaspoons Thai yellow curry paste

2 teaspoons fish sauce

3 teaspoons soy sauce

½ teaspoon Truvia or Swerve

5 scallions, chopped, divided

4 garlic cloves, crushed

1 (2-inch) piece fresh ginger, finely chopped

1 (15-ounce) can straw mushrooms with their liquid (optional)

½ cup grape tomato halves

¼ cup chopped fresh cilantro

Juice of 1 lime

¼ cup chopped cashews

PREP TIME
10 minutes

SOUP
12 minutes high pressure

RELEASE
Quick

TOTAL TIME
35 minutes

MACROS
64% Fat
6% Carbs
30% Protein

DAIRY-FREE

UNDER 45 MINUTES

1. Put the chicken thighs in the inner cooking pot of the Instant Pot®. Add the coconut milk, curry paste, fish sauce, soy sauce, Truvia or Swerve, half the scallions, garlic, and ginger. Stir to combine.

2. Lock the lid into place. Select Soup and adjust the pressure to High (the Soup setting prevents the coconut milk from boiling and separating). Cook for 12 minutes. When the cooking is complete, quick-release the pressure. Unlock the lid.

3. Use tongs to transfer the chicken to a bowl. Shred the chicken, then stir it back into the soup.

4. Stir in the straw mushrooms (if using), tomatoes, the remaining half of the scallions, cilantro, and lime juice. Let the vegetables heat through, then serve topped with cashews.

Per Serving Calories: 344; Total Fat: 24g; Total Carbs: 9g; Net Carbs: 7g; Fiber: 2g; Sugar: 4g; Protein: 22g

Chiken and Kale Soup

SERVES 4

Make this delicious chicken and kale soup with leftover cooked chicken, kale, and warm winter spices in your Instant Pot® for a soul-satisfying, low-carb soup that's perfect for cold winter nights. The mix of spices might sound odd, but do you know what I really find odd? It's that children seem to love this soup, green things and all.

2 cups chopped cooked chicken breast

12 ounces frozen kale

1 onion, chopped

2 cups water

1 tablespoon powdered chicken broth base

½ teaspoon ground cinnamon

Pinch ground cloves

2 teaspoons minced garlic

1 teaspoon freshly ground black pepper

1 teaspoon salt

2 cups full-fat coconut milk

PREP TIME
5 minutes

PRESSURE COOK/MANUAL
5 minutes high pressure

RELEASE
Natural 10 minutes, then Quick

TOTAL TIME
30 minutes

MACROS
64% Fat
10% Carbs
26% Protein

DAIRY-FREE

GLUTEN-FREE

POUR AND COOK

UNDER 45 MINUTES

1. Put the chicken, kale, onion, water, chicken broth base, cinnamon, cloves, garlic, pepper, and salt in the inner cooking pot of the Instant Pot®.

2. Lock the lid into place. Select Manual or Pressure Cook and adjust the pressure to High. Cook for 5 minutes. When the cooking is complete, let the pressure release naturally for 10 minutes, then quick-release any remaining pressure. Unlock the lid.

3. Stir in the coconut milk. Taste and adjust any seasonings as needed before serving.

Per Serving Calories: 387; Total Fat: 27g; Total Carbs: 10g; Net Carbs: 8g; Fiber: 2g; Sugar: 2g; Protein: 26g;

TIP: *The cinnamon and cloves taste should be well balanced. You don't want people to go, "Mmm, cloves!" since we aren't making dessert here. You just want them to go, "Mmm, soup!"*

Savory Chicken and Mushroom Soup

SERVES 4

This creamy mushroom and chicken soup is full of protein and flavor, and is a great pour and cook (mostly) recipe. I find this to be a hearty and comforting soup, and the fact that it needs just a few ingredients is a bonus. The flavor payoff is much more than you'd expect with such a humble set of ingredients.

1 onion, cut into thin slices

3 garlic cloves, minced

2 cups chopped mushrooms

1 yellow summer squash, chopped

1 pound boneless, skinless chicken breast, cut into large chunks

2½ cups chicken broth

1 teaspoon salt

1 teaspoon freshly ground black pepper

1 teaspoon Italian seasoning or poultry seasoning

1 cup heavy (whipping) cream

PREP TIME
5 minutes

PRESSURE COOK/MANUAL
15 minutes high pressure

RELEASE
Natural 10 minutes, then Quick

TOTAL TIME
40 minutes

MACROS
60% Fat
11% Carbs
29% Protein

GLUTEN-FREE

SOY-FREE

UNDER 45 MINUTES

1. Put the onion, garlic, mushrooms, squash, chicken, chicken broth, salt, pepper, and Italian seasoning in the inner cooking pot of the Instant Pot®.

2. Lock the lid into place. Select Manual or Pressure Cook and adjust the pressure to High. Cook for 15 minutes. When the cooking is complete, let the pressure release naturally for 10 minutes, then quick-release any remaining pressure. Unlock the lid.

3. Using tongs, transfer the chicken pieces to a bowl and set aside.

4. Tilt the pot slightly. Using an immersion blender, roughly purée the vegetables, leaving a few intact for texture and visual appeal.

5. Shred the chicken and stir it back in to the soup.

6. Add the cream and stir well. Serve.

Per Serving Calories: 427; Total Fat: 28g; Total Carbs: 13g; Net Carbs: 11g; Fiber: 2g; Sugar: 5g; Protein: 31g

4

Seafood and Poultry

Savory Shrimp with Tomatoes and Feta, page 74

Creamy Shrimp Scampi

SERVES 6

Talk about quick and easy! Keto shrimp scampi from your Instant Pot® cooks in no time and may become one of your go-to meals, especially when you need something fast. Serve it on top of zoodles for a quick dinner. This rich and creamy dish is sure to satisfy. Just make sure to use frozen shrimp, or the shrimp will overcook.

2 tablespoons unsalted butter

4 garlic cloves, minced

¼ teaspoon red pepper flakes, or to taste

½ teaspoon smoked paprika

1 pound frozen peeled shrimp

½ to 1 teaspoon salt

1 teaspoon freshly ground black pepper

½ cup water or chicken broth

½ cup heavy (whipping) cream

½ cup Parmesan cheese

2 cups cooked zucchini noodles

PREP TIME
5 minutes

SAUTÉ
1 minute, plus 1 minute after pressure cooking

PRESSURE COOK/MANUAL
2 minutes high pressure

RELEASE
Quick

TOTAL TIME
20 minutes

MACROS
60% Fat
4% Carbs
36% Protein

GLUTEN-FREE

SOY-FREE

UNDER 45 MINUTES

1. Preheat the Instant Pot® by selecting Sauté and adjusting to high heat. When the inner cooking pot is hot, add the butter and heat until it foams. Add the garlic and red pepper flakes and sauté until the garlic is slightly browned, 1 to 2 minutes.

2. Add the paprika and then the frozen shrimp, salt, and pepper.

3. Pour in the water or broth. If using water, add ½ teaspoon of salt.

4. Lock the lid into place. Select Manual or Pressure Cook and adjust the pressure to High. Cook for 2 minutes. When the cooking is complete, quick-release the pressure immediately. Unlock and remove the lid.

5. Turn the pot to Sauté and adjust to high heat. Add the cream and cheese, and stir until melted and combined, about 1 minute.

6. Portion the zucchini noodles in individual bowls or plates, and then top each one with the creamy shrimp scampi. Serve immediately.

Per Serving Calories: 332; Total Fat: 23g; Total Carbs: 4g; Net Carbs: 4g; Fiber: 0g; Sugar: 0g; Protein: 28g

Chinese-Style Steamed Ginger Scallion Fish

SERVES 4

It is indeed possible to make the most delectable, flaky fish in your Instant Pot®—if you know what you're doing. Using a pot-in-pot method or a steamer is key to the success of this recipe, as it uses low pressure. If your Instant Pot® doesn't have a low pressure adjustment, reduce cooking time by a minute and see how it does for you.

1 pound frozen tilapia fillets

3 tablespoons soy sauce

2 tablespoons rice wine

1 tablespoon doubanjiang (see page 13)

1 teaspoon minced fresh ginger

1 teaspoon minced garlic

3 tablespoons peanut oil

2 tablespoons julienned fresh ginger, divided (see Tip)

¼ cup julienned scallions

¼ cup chopped fresh cilantro

PREP TIME
10 minutes

PRESSURE COOK/MANUAL
2 minutes low pressure

RELEASE
Quick

TOTAL TIME
25 minutes + 30 minutes marinating time

MACROS
54% Fat
3% Carbs
43% Protein

DAIRY-FREE

1. Place the fish fillets on a rimmed plate or in a shallow bowl. In a small bowl, mix together the soy sauce, rice wine, doubanjiang, minced ginger, and garlic. Pour this over the fish and let it marinate for 20 to 30 minutes. If you marinate for longer than 30 minutes, cover the bowl and refrigerate it.

2. Remove the fish from the marinade and place it in a steamer basket. Reserve the marinade.

3. Pour 2 cups of water into the inner cooking pot of the Instant Pot®. Place the steamer basket over the water. Lock the lid into place. Select Manual or Pressure Cook and adjust the pressure to Low. Cook for 2 minutes. When the cooking is complete, quick-release the pressure. Unlock the lid.

4. While the fish cooks, place a saucepan over medium-high heat and add the oil. Once the oil shimmers, add the julienned ginger and sauté for 10 seconds. Add the scallions and cilantro, and stir-fry for about 2 minutes, or until softened. Add the reserved marinade and let this boil vigorously until cooked through.

5. Divide the fish between serving plates. Pour the sauce over the fish and serve immediately.

Per Serving Calories: 185; Total Fat: 10g; Total Carbs: 2g; Net Carbs: 2g; Fiber: 0g; Sugar: 0g; Protein: 24g

TIP: *To julienne ginger easily, cut it sideways into circles. Stack the circles together, and cut into long matchsticks.*

Easy Lobster Bisque

SERVES 4

There are times when you want a treat or something truly special. Lobster bisque certainly fits that bill. Traditional lobster bisque is a labor-intensive production. Enter the Instant Pot®. You can make this rave-worthy bisque in far less time with equally delicious results. It's a great recipe to put together for your next dinner party.

---

2 teaspoons Ghee (page 150) or unsalted butter

1 onion, chopped

1 tablespoon minced garlic

1 tablespoon minced fresh ginger

2 cups chicken broth

1 cup chopped tomatoes

3 cups chopped cauliflower

2 tablespoons ready-made pesto

½ teaspoon salt (or more, depending on how salty your pesto and broth are)

1 to 2 teaspoons freshly ground black pepper

1 pound cooked lobster meat (or shrimp or crab meat)

1 cup heavy (whipping) cream

PREP TIME
10 minutes

SAUTÉ
3 minutes, plus 1 minute after pressure cooking

PRESSURE COOK/MANUAL
4 minutes high pressure

RELEASE
Natural 10 minutes, then Quick

TOTAL TIME
40 minutes

MACROS
60% Fat
14% Carbs
26% Protein

GLUTEN-FREE

SOY-FREE

UNDER 45 MINUTES

1. Preheat the Instant Pot® by selecting Sauté and adjusting to high heat. When the inner cooking pot is hot, add the ghee and heat until it is shimmering. Add the onion, garlic, and ginger. Sauté until softened, 2 to 3 minutes.

2. Pour in the chicken broth and stir, scraping the bottom of the pan to loosen any browned bits. Add the tomatoes, cauliflower, pesto, salt, and pepper.

3. Lock the lid into place. Select Manual or Pressure Cook and adjust the pressure to High. Cook for 4 minutes. When the cooking is complete, let the pressure release naturally for 10 minutes, then quick-release any remaining pressure. Unlock the lid.

4. Tilting the pot, use an immersion blender to purée the vegetables into a smooth soup.

5. Turn the pot to Sauté and adjust to high heat. Add the lobster meat and cook until it is heated through. Stir in the cream and serve.

Per Serving Calories: 441; Total Fat: 30g; Total Carbs: 14g; Net Carbs: 10g; Fiber: 4g; Sugar: 5g; Protein: 30g

TIP: *Ghee is the ideal ingredient to use in this recipe and is a staple of the keto diet. In a pinch, you can use the same amount of butter in a recipe.*

Sesame-Ginger Chicken

SERVES 6

Recipes like this one and the Chicken Shawarma (page 94) are a good starting point for learning how to make richly flavored meats that are not soups or stews. Salads, for example: I have yet to meet a chicken salad with peanuts that I don't love, and I mean LOVE. This recipe produces an incredibly flavorful chicken that can be eaten in a lovely, crunchy salad with my Easy Asian Peanut Dressing (page 156), as pictured.

1½ pounds boneless, skinless chicken thighs, cut into large pieces

2 tablespoons soy sauce

1 tablespoon sesame oil

1 tablespoon minced fresh ginger

1 tablespoon minced garlic

1 tablespoon Truvia

1 tablespoon rice vinegar

PREP TIME
5 minutes

PRESSURE COOK/MANUAL
10 minutes high pressure

RELEASE
Natural 10 minutes, then Quick

TOTAL TIME
35 minutes

MACROS
66% Fat
6% Carbs
28% Protein

DAIRY-FREE

UNDER 45 MINUTES

1. Put the chicken in a heatproof bowl. Add the soy sauce, sesame oil, ginger, garlic, Truvia, and vinegar. Stir to coat the chicken. Cover the bowl with aluminum foil or a silicone lid.

2. Pour 2 cups of water into the inner cooking pot of the Instant Pot®, then place a trivet in the pot. Place the bowl on the trivet.

3. Lock the lid into place. Select Manual or Pressure Cook and adjust the pressure to High. Cook for 10 minutes. When the cooking is complete, let the pressure release naturally for 10 minutes, then quick-release any remaining pressure. Unlock the lid.

4. Remove the chicken and shred it, then mix it back in with the liquid in the bowl.

5. Serve as is, over zoodles, or in a salad, as shown on the opposite page, with crushed peanuts and Easy Asian Peanut Dressing (page 156).

Per Serving Calories: 272; Total Fat: 20g; Total Carbs: 4g; Net Carbs: 4g; Fiber: 0g; Sugar: 3g; Protein: 19g

Savory Shrimp with Tomatoes and Feta

SERVES 6

This is a lovely, easy dish starring shrimp, tomatoes, feta, and olives—a classic combination if there ever was one. Best of all, it requires almost no effort. A quick sauté right in the Instant Pot®, add the shrimp, and cook. You can pour yourself a drink while you wait for this quick and tasty dinner, although it will be ready after you have only a sip or two—it's that fast.

3 tablespoons unsalted butter

1 tablespoon garlic

½ teaspoon red pepper flakes, or more as needed

1½ cups chopped onion

1 (14.5-ounce) can diced tomatoes, undrained

1 teaspoon dried oregano

1 teaspoon salt

1 pound frozen shrimp (21–25 count), peeled

1 cup crumbled feta cheese

½ cup sliced black olives

¼ cup chopped parsley

PREP TIME
10 minutes

SAUTÉ
1 minute

PRESSURE COOK/MANUAL
1 minute low pressure

RELEASE
Quick

TOTAL TIME
25 minutes

MACROS
55% Fat
12% Carbs
33% Protein

GLUTEN-FREE

SOY-FREE

UNDER 45 MINUTES

1. Preheat the Instant Pot® by selecting Sauté and adjusting to high heat. When the inner cooking pot is hot, add the butter and heat until it foams. Add the garlic and red pepper flakes, and cook just until fragrant, about 1 minute.

2. Add the onion, tomatoes, oregano, and salt, and stir to combine.

3. Add the frozen shrimp.

4. Lock the lid into place. Select Manual or Pressure Cook and adjust the pressure to Low. Cook for 1 minute. When the cooking is complete, quick-release the pressure. Unlock the lid.

5. Mix the shrimp in with the lovely tomato broth.

6. Allow the mixture to cool slightly. Right before serving, sprinkle with the feta cheese, olives, and parsley. This dish makes a soupy broth, so it's great over mashed cauliflower.

Per Serving Calories: 361; Total Fat: 22g; Total Carbs: 13g; Net Carbs: 11g; Fiber: 2g; Sugar: 2g; Protein: 30g

Chicken Bratwurst Meatballs with Cabbage

SERVES 4

How cool is it to make bratwurst at home? Or at least bratwurst meatballs. This easy chicken sausage recipe makes meatballs that are very mildly spiced but flavorful, and sure to be very kid-friendly. I use ground chicken, but use whatever works for you. I also admit I find it cool that I can make meatballs in the Instant Pot®.

1 pound ground chicken

¼ cup heavy (whipping) cream

2 teaspoons salt, divided

½ teaspoon ground caraway seeds

1½ teaspoons freshly ground black pepper, divided

¼ teaspoon ground allspice

4 to 6 cups thickly chopped green cabbage

½ cup milk

2 tablespoons unsalted butter

PREP TIME
15 minutes

PRESSURE COOK/MANUAL
4 minutes high pressure

RELEASE
Quick

TOTAL TIME
30 minutes, plus 30 minutes to chill

MACROS
62% Fat
11% Carbs
27% Protein

GLUTEN-FREE

1. To make the meatballs, put the chicken in a bowl. Add the cream, 1 teaspoon of salt, the caraway, ½ teaspoon of pepper, and the allspice. Mix thoroughly. Refrigerate the mixture for 30 minutes. Once the mixture has cooled, it is easier to form the meatballs.

2. Using a small scoop, form the chicken mixture into small- to medium-size meatballs. Place half the meatballs in the inner cooking pot of your Instant Pot® and cover them with half the cabbage. Place the remaining meatballs on top of the cabbage, then cover them with the rest of the cabbage.

3. Pour in the milk, place pats of the butter here and there, and sprinkle with the remaining 1 teaspoon of salt and 1 teaspoon of pepper.

4. Lock the lid into place. Select Manual or Pressure Cook and adjust the pressure to High. Cook for 4 minutes. When the cooking is complete, quick-release the pressure. Unlock the lid.

5. Serve the meatballs on top of the cabbage.

Per Serving Calories: 338; Total Fat: 23g; Total Carbs: 10g; Net Carbs: 7g; Fiber: 3g; Sugar: 2g; Protein: 23g

TIP: You can substitute ground beef or pork for the chicken; just check the internal temperature to ensure they're cooked through. You can also broil or air fry the bratwurst meatballs at the end for a browner look.

Shortcut Dan Dan–Style Chicken

SERVES 4

I love Sichuan food, but it's a 45-minute drive for me to get to the good stuff. Luckily, I make a super-tasty Sichuan Pork Soup (page 48). But dan dan mein is something else, as the noodles are definitely not keto-friendly. With a little trial and error, I developed this recipe where you make a sauce and cook the chicken with it.

2 tablespoons creamy peanut butter

1 tablespoon doubanjiang (see page 13)

2 teaspoons soy sauce

2 teaspoons rice wine vinegar

½ to 2 teaspoons red pepper flakes

1 teaspoon ground Sichuan peppercorns

¼ cup hot water

1 pound boneless, skinless chicken breast or thighs, cut into bite-size pieces

¼ cup room-temperature water

1 (8-ounce) package shirataki noodles, rinsed

1 tablespoon sesame oil

¼ cup chopped peanuts

¼ cup chopped fresh cilantro (optional)

PREP TIME
5 minutes

PRESSURE COOK/MANUAL
7 minutes high pressure

RELEASE
Natural 10 minutes, then Quick

TOTAL TIME
40 minutes, plus 30 minutes to marinate

MACROS
53% Fat
12% Carbs
35% Protein

DAIRY-FREE

1. In a medium bowl, mix together the peanut butter, doubanjiang, soy sauce, vinegar, red pepper flakes, peppercorns, and hot water.

2. Put the chicken in the bowl and mix so the chicken is well coated. For the best results, let the chicken marinate for 30 minutes.

3. Put the chicken and marinade in the inner cooking pot of the Instant Pot®. Pour in the room-temperature water.

4. Lock the lid into place. Select Manual or Pressure Cook and adjust the pressure to High. Cook for 7 minutes. When the cooking is complete, let the pressure release naturally for 10 minutes, then quick-release any remaining pressure. Unlock the lid.

5. While the chicken is cooking, prepare the shirataki noodles according to the package instructions.

6. Mix the chicken with the noodles. Just before serving, stir in the sesame oil. Serve garnished with the peanuts and cilantro (if using).

Per Serving Calories: 297; Total Fat: 17g; Total Carbs: 10g; Net Carbs: 5g; Fiber: 5g; Sugar: 3g; Protein: 26g

West African Peanut Stew

There are many different ways to make this groundnut stew. The only constant is veggies and peanut butter, with everything else being up to the cook to decide. Try it this way once, and then you can mix and match to your heart's content.

1 cup chopped onion

2 tablespoons minced garlic

1 tablespoon minced fresh ginger

1 teaspoon salt

½ teaspoon ground cumin

½ teaspoon ground coriander

½ teaspoon freshly ground black pepper

½ teaspoon ground cinnamon

⅛ teaspoon ground cloves

1 tablespoon tomato paste

1 pound boneless, skinless chicken breasts or thighs, cut into large chunks

3 to 4 cups chopped Swiss chard

1 cup cubed raw pumpkin

½ cup water

1 cup chunky peanut butter

PREP TIME
10 minutes

PRESSURE COOK/MANUAL
10 minutes high pressure

RELEASE
Natural

TOTAL TIME
50 minutes

MACROS
60% Fat
10% Carbs
30% Protein

DAIRY-FREE

GLUTEN-FREE

SOY-FREE

POUR AND COOK

1. In the inner cooking pot of the Instant Pot®, stir together the onion, garlic, ginger, salt, cumin, coriander, pepper, cinnamon, cloves, and tomato paste. Add the chicken, chard, pumpkin, and water.

2. Lock the lid into place. Select Manual or Pressure Cook and adjust the pressure to High. Cook for 10 minutes. When the cooking is complete, let the pressure release naturally. Unlock the lid.

3. Mix in the peanut butter a little at a time. Taste with each addition, as your reward for cooking. The final sauce should be thick enough to coat the back of a spoon in a thin layer.

4. Serve over mashed cauliflower, cooked zucchini noodles, steamed vegetables, or with a side salad.

Per Serving Calories: 411; Total Fat: 27g; Total Carbs: 15g; Net Carbs: 10g; Fiber: 5g; Sugar: 5g; Protein: 31g

Now and Later Butter Chicken

SERVES 4

When I first made my now-famous butter chicken, all I focused on was getting the easiest and best butter chicken I could. Despite years of cooking keto, it didn't occur to me until much later that this recipe was fabulously keto-friendly. But that epitomizes what good keto cooking should be: taste first, normal everyday ingredients where possible, and macros that align. This recipe does make twice the amount of sauce the chicken needs, although opinions are divided on this. The rather large contingent of sauce drinkers argue it's not enough sauce, but the chicken agrees with me—there's plenty of sauce to save and use with shrimp, fish, or cooked meats, or on top of fried eggs.

1 (14.5-ounce) can diced tomatoes, undrained

5 or 6 garlic cloves, minced

1 tablespoon minced fresh ginger

1 teaspoon ground turmeric

1 teaspoon cayenne

1 teaspoon smoked paprika

2 teaspoons Garam Masala (page 151), divided

1 teaspoon ground cumin

1 teaspoon salt

1 pound boneless, skinless chicken breasts or thighs

½ cup unsalted butter, cut into cubes, or ½ cup coconut oil

½ cup heavy (whipping) cream or full-fat coconut milk

¼ to ½ cup chopped fresh cilantro

4 cups Cauliflower Rice (page 149) or cucumber noodles

PREP TIME
15 minutes

SAUTÉ
5 minutes

PRESSURE COOK/MANUAL
10 minutes high pressure

RELEASE
Natural

TOTAL TIME
55 minutes

MACROS
63% Fat
13% Carbs
24% Protein

GLUTEN-FREE

1. Put the tomatoes, garlic, ginger, turmeric, cayenne, paprika, 1 teaspoon of garam masala, cumin, and salt in the inner cooking pot of the Instant Pot®. Mix thoroughly, then place the chicken pieces on top of the sauce.

2. Lock the lid into place. Select Manual and adjust the pressure to High. Cook for 10 minutes. When the cooking is complete, let the pressure release naturally. Unlock the lid. Carefully remove the chicken and set aside.

3. Using an immersion blender in the pot, blend together all the ingredients into a smooth sauce. (Or use a stand blender, but be careful with the hot sauce and be sure to leave the inside lid open to vent.) After blending, let the sauce cool before adding the remaining ingredients or it will be thinner than is ideal.

4. Add the butter cubes, cream, remaining 1 teaspoon of garam masala, and cilantro. Stir until well incorporated. The sauce should be thick enough to coat the back of a spoon when you're done.

5. Remove half the sauce and freeze it for later or refrigerate for up to 2 to 3 days.

6. Cut the chicken into bite-size pieces. Add it back to the sauce.

7. Preheat the Instant Pot® by selecting Sauté and adjust to Less for low heat. Let the chicken heat through. Break it up into smaller pieces if you like, but don't shred it.

8. Serve over cauliflower rice or raw cucumber noodles.

Per Serving Calories: 512; Total Fat: 36g; Total Carbs: 16g; Net Carbs: 10g; Fiber: 6g; Sugar: 7g; Protein: 31g

TIP: *To make this dish later with the extra sauce, use leftover cooked chicken and mix it in with the gently heated sauce, let it simmer for a few minutes for the flavors to meld together, and there you go. Add the cilantro on top.*

Sweet and Spicy Chicken Tinga

SERVES 6

Instant Pot® chicken tinga is a sweet, spicy, and utterly delicious authentic Mexican dish. I know there are as many chicken tinga recipes out there as there are cooks, and this is how I make mine. It may not match your abuela's tinga, but it tastes great and it tastes like real Mexican food, and that's good enough for me!

4 teaspoons vegetable oil

2 tomatillos, cut into thin slices

½ onion, cut into thin slices

3 garlic cloves

1 (14.5-ounce) can fire-roasted tomatoes

⅓ cup chicken broth

1 chipotle chile with adobo sauce from a can, chopped

½ teaspoon ground cumin

¼ teaspoon ground cinnamon

½ teaspoon dried oregano

1 teaspoon Truvia or Swerve

1 tablespoon fish sauce or soy sauce (see Tip)

1 tablespoon cider vinegar

1½ pounds boneless, skinless chicken thighs

½ cup sour cream

½ cup buttermilk or 2 teaspoons lemon juice

1 avocado, sliced

PREP TIME
10 minutes

SAUTÉ
15 minutes

PRESSURE COOK/MANUAL
15 minutes

RELEASE
Natural 10 minutes, then Quick

TOTAL TIME
1 hour

MACROS
56% Fat
8% Carbs
36% Protein

1. Preheat the Instant Pot® by selecting Sauté and adjusting to high heat. When the inner cooking pot is hot, add the oil and heat until it is shimmering.

2. Add the tomatillo slices in a single layer, then add the onions in as flat a layer as possible between the tomatillo slices. Nestle in the garlic cloves. You're going to let these char, so do not stir them.

3. Once the thinner slices start to look a little burned, flip the vegetables. The bottom of the pot will have large black spots where the vegetables have charred, but this is a good thing.

4. Once the vegetables are well charred, add the tomatoes and broth and deglaze the pan, scraping up all the lovely brown bits from the bottom. Do this really well and ensure there are no burned bits remaining on the bottom. Otherwise, your Instant Pot® will not come to pressure.

5. Add the chipotle, cumin, cinnamon, oregano, sweetener, fish sauce, and vinegar. Cook for 1 to 2 minutes to allow the spices to bloom. Add the chicken.

6. Lock the lid into place. Select Manual or Pressure Cook and adjust the pressure to High. Cook for 15 minutes. When the pressure cooking is complete, let the pressure release naturally for 10 minutes, then quick-release any remaining pressure. Unlock the lid.

7. Remove the chicken and shred it.

8. Tilting the pot, use an immersion blender to purée the sauce until the mixture is smooth.

9. Turn the pot to Sauté and adjust to high heat, then cook to thicken the sauce for about 10 minutes. Once it's thickened a bit, add in the chicken and heat through.

10. While the chicken heats, make crema in a small bowl by mixing together the sour cream and buttermilk. (If you do not have buttermilk, use lemon juice instead.)

11. Top the chicken with the crema and avocado slices. Serve over cauliflower rice, or wrapped in lettuce leaves for a low-carb option. You can also use low-carb corn tortillas.

TIP: *Before you write to me in droves, yes, I know fish sauce is not traditional in Mexican cooking. But it does add a wonderful, meaty richness to this tinga, and it tastes better with it. As my readers would write: #trusturvashi.*

Per Serving Calories: 260; Total Fat: 16g; Total Carbs: 9g; Net Carbs: 6g; Fiber: 3g; Sugar: 4g; Protein: 24g

Mexican-Style Chicken with Red Salsa

SERVES 8

This simple yet flavorful chicken will add great pizzazz to your dinner table. It's fast, delicious, and extremely flavorful. You're going to feel like you're adding waaaay too many spices—but you're not. You're adding just the right amount, and the dish is going to be spectacular when you're done. It's one of those super-easy recipes where you do minimal browning, then throw everything in the Instant Pot® and just let it cook. Add fat, if desired, by topping with Cheddar cheese and avocado.

2 pounds boneless, skinless chicken thighs, cut into bite-size pieces

1½ tablespoons ground cumin

1½ tablespoons chili powder

1 tablespoon salt

2 tablespoons vegetable oil

1 (14.5-ounce) can diced tomatoes, undrained

1 (5-ounce) can tomato paste

1 small onion, chopped

3 garlic cloves, minced

2 ounces pickled jalapeños from a can, with juice

½ cup sour cream

PREP TIME
10 minutes

SAUTÉ
5 minutes

PRESSURE COOK/MANUAL
15 minutes high pressure

RELEASE
Natural 10 minutes, then Quick

TOTAL TIME
50 minutes

MACROS
66% Fat
8% Carbs
26% Protein

GLUTEN-FREE

SOY-FREE

1. Preheat the Instant Pot® by selecting Sauté and adjusting to high heat.

2. In a medium bowl, coat the chicken with the cumin, chili powder, and salt.

3. Put the oil in the inner cooking pot. When it is shimmering, add the coated chicken pieces. (This step lets the spices bloom a bit to get their full flavor.) Cook the chicken for 4 to 5 minutes. ➤

4. Add the tomatoes, tomato paste, onion, garlic, and jalapeños.

5. Lock the lid into place. Select Manual or Pressure Cook and adjust the pressure to High. Cook for 15 minutes. When the cooking is complete, let the pressure release naturally for 10 minutes, then quick-release any remaining pressure. Unlock and remove the lid.

6. Use two forks to shred the chicken. Serve topped with the sour cream. This dish is good with mashed cauliflower, steamed vegetables, or a salad.

Per Serving Calories: 329; Total Fat: 24g; Total Carbs: 8g; Net Carbs: 6g; Fiber: 2g; Sugar: 5g; Protein: 21g

Thai Green Curry

SERVES 6

Yes, you can slow cook in your Instant Pot®! This Thai curry with chicken and vegetables makes a fragrant, aromatic dish that hits the spot. I did try to make this under pressure, and it was quite thin and soupy when compared to the richness of the sauce when slow cooked.

1 tablespoon coconut oil

2 tablespoons Thai green curry paste (adjust to your preferred spice level)

1 tablespoon minced fresh ginger

1 tablespoon minced garlic

½ cup sliced onion

1 pound boneless, skinless chicken thighs

2 cups peeled, chopped eggplant

1 cup chopped green, yellow, or orange bell pepper

½ cup fresh basil leaves, preferably Thai basil

1½ cups unsweetened coconut milk

1 tablespoon fish sauce

2 tablespoons soy sauce

2 teaspoons Truvia or Swerve

Salt

PREP TIME
10 minutes

SAUTÉ
3 minutes

SLOW COOK
8 hours medium

TOTAL TIME
8 hours 15 minutes

MACROS
62% Fat
15% Carbs
23% Protein

DAIRY-FREE

TIP: *Substitute yellow or red curry pastes for a change of pace and heat.*

1. Preheat the Instant Pot® by selecting Sauté and adjusting to high heat. When the inner cooking pot is hot, add the coconut oil and heat until it is shimmering. Add the curry paste and cook for 1 to 2 minutes, stirring occasionally.

2. Add the ginger and garlic and stir-fry for 30 seconds. Add the onion and stir it all together.

3. Add the chicken, eggplant, bell pepper, basil, coconut milk, fish sauce, soy sauce, and Truvia or Swerve. Stir to combine.

4. Press Cancel to turn off Sauté mode, and switch to Slow Cook mode. Adjust to cook for 8 hours on medium (not low).

5. When the curry has finished cooking, add salt to taste.

Per Serving Calories: 290; Total Fat: 20g; Total Carbs: 12g; Net Carbs: 9g; Fiber: 3g; Sugar: 5g; Protein: 17g

Chicken Tikka Masala

SERVES 6

Ask six people if they know who invented chicken tikka masala, and you'll get six different answers. Really, given the amount of "discussion" (i.e., heated arguments) around the origins of this dish, you'd think we were arguing about a discovery that would qualify for a Nobel Prize! Here's what I suggest: Get yourself a hearty bowl of this dish and eat it as you watch other people argue about whether this dish is Indian, British, Bangladeshi, Persian, or none of the above.

FOR THE MARINADE

½ cup Greek yogurt

4 garlic cloves, minced

2 teaspoons minced fresh ginger

½ teaspoon ground turmeric

¼ teaspoon cayenne

½ teaspoon smoked paprika

1 teaspoon salt

1 teaspoon Garam Masala (page 151)

½ teaspoon ground cumin

1 teaspoon liquid smoke (optional)

1½ pounds boneless, skinless chicken breasts or thighs, cut into large pieces

FOR THE SAUCE

1 onion, chopped

1 (14-ounce) can diced tomatoes, undrained

1 carrot, chopped

5 garlic cloves, minced

2 teaspoons minced fresh ginger

1 teaspoon ground turmeric

½ teaspoon cayenne

1 teaspoon smoked paprika

1 teaspoon salt

2 teaspoons Garam Masala (page 151)

1 teaspoon ground cumin

FOR FINISHING THE DISH

1 cup heavy (whipping) cream or full-fat coconut milk

1 teaspoon Garam Masala (page 151)

¼ to ½ cup chopped fresh cilantro

PREP TIME
20 minutes, plus 1 to 2 hours to marinate

PRESSURE COOK/MANUAL
10 minutes high pressure

RELEASE
Quick

TOTAL TIME
40 minutes, plus time to marinate

MACROS
60% Fat
9% Carbs
31% Protein

GLUTEN-FREE

SOY-FREE

To make the marinade

In a large bowl, mix together the yogurt, garlic, ginger, turmeric, cayenne, paprika, salt, garam masala, cumin, and liquid smoke (if using). Add the chicken and stir to coat. Marinate the chicken for 1 to 2 hours in the refrigerator.

To make the sauce

1. In the inner cooking pot of the Instant Pot®, mix the onion, tomatoes, carrot, garlic, ginger, turmeric, cayenne, paprika, salt, garam masala, and cumin. Place the chicken with the yogurt on top of the sauce ingredients.

2. Lock the lid into place. Select Manual or Pressure Cook and adjust the pressure to High. Cook for 10 minutes. When the cooking is complete, quick-release the pressure. Unlock and remove the lid.

3. Remove the chicken and set aside. (If you like, you can brown it under the broiler or in an air fryer at this point.)

4. Tilting the pot, use an immersion blender to purée the sauce well.

To finish the dish

1. Add the cream and garam masala to the sauce and stir well.

2. Remove half the sauce and freeze for later.

3. Put the chicken back into the remaining sauce. Garnish with the cilantro and serve.

Per Serving Calories: 366; Total Fat: 24g; Total Carbs: 10g; Net Carbs: 8g; Fiber: 2g; Sugar: 4g; Protein: 29g

TIP: *The spices for marinating and for the sauce are almost the same. To save time, you can add the marinade spices to a bowl and the sauce spices to the Instant Pot® at the same time.*

Chicken Vindaloo

SERVES 4

This dish is said to have originated when Portuguese soldiers invaded India and brought with them a combination of preserved ingredients—pork layered with garlic and wine. Over time, Indian cooks added chiles to both season and preserve the meats, and then cooks like me, that breed of people who are congenitally incapable of making a recipe as directed, tinkered until we have what is now referred to as a "vindaloo." Of course, there are many ways to make a good vindaloo, but this is one of the better ones. Adjust the cayenne pepper to suit your spice preference.

1 cup diced onion

5 garlic cloves, minced

1 tablespoon minced fresh ginger

1 tablespoon peanut oil

¼ cup white vinegar

1 cup canned diced tomatoes, with their juices

1 teaspoon salt

1 teaspoon Garam Masala (page 151)

1 teaspoon smoked paprika

½ teaspoon cayenne

½ teaspoon ground coriander

½ teaspoon ground cumin

1 pound boneless, skinless chicken thighs

¼ cup water

½ teaspoon ground turmeric

PREP TIME
15 minutes, plus up to 8 hours to marinate

COOK TIME
7 minutes

PRESSURE COOK/MANUAL
5 minutes high pressure

RELEASE
Natural 10 minutes, then Quick

TOTAL TIME
50 minutes, plus time to marinate

MACROS
38% Fat
13% Carbs
49% Protein

DAIRY-FREE

GLUTEN-FREE

SOY-FREE

1. In a large microwave-safe bowl, combine the onion, garlic, ginger, and oil. Heat in the microwave on full power for 5 to 7 minutes, until the vegetables are browned on the edges.

2. Transfer the onion mixture to a blender jar. Add the vinegar, tomatoes, salt, garam masala, paprika, cayenne, coriander, and cumin. Blend into a smooth paste.

3. Place the chicken in the heatproof bowl you used earlier, and spoon the spice and vegetable mix over it, mixing well to coat the chicken. Pour the water into the blender and pulse briefly to rinse out the remaining spices. Pour the spiced water over the chicken.

4. Add the turmeric and stir to combine (adding it earlier could stain your blender jar). Cover the bowl and marinate the chicken for 30 minutes or up to 8 hours. (If you marinate it for longer than 30 minutes, refrigerate the chicken.)

5. Pour the chicken and marinade into the inner cooking pot of the Instant Pot®. Lock the lid into place. Select Manual or Pressure Cook and adjust the pressure to High. Cook for 5 minutes. When the cooking is complete, let the pressure release naturally for 10 minutes, then quick-release any remaining pressure. Unlock and remove the lid.

6. If the sauce is too thin, select Sauté and adjust to More for high heat. Remove the chicken pieces and bring the sauce to a boil to evaporate some of the excess water. Return the chicken to the sauce and serve.

Per Serving Calories: 188; Total Fat: 8g; Total Carbs: 6g; Net Carbs: 4g; Fiber: 2g; Sugar: 2g; Protein: 23g

Chicken Shawarma

SERVES 4

This chicken shawarma is fantastic and needs just a few spices. I love finding uses for my Shawarma Spice Mix (page 152), because a few easily available spices are all you need to create a new dish. The combination is a great flavor that kids love, too. Try this dish, and you might find yourself licking your plate clean.

1 pound boneless, skinless chicken thighs or breasts, cut into large bite-size chunks

3 teaspoons extra-virgin olive oil, divided

3 tablespoons Shawarma Spice Mix (page 152)

1 cup thinly sliced onions

¼ cup water

4 large lettuce leaves

1 cup Tzatziki Sauce (page 154)

PREP TIME
10 minutes, plus up to 24 hours to marinate

SAUTÉ
4 minutes

PRESSURE COOK/MANUAL
10 minutes high pressure

RELEASE
Quick

TOTAL TIME
35 minutes, plus time to marinate

MACROS
51% Fat
7% Carbs
42% Protein

GLUTEN-FREE

SOY-FREE

TIP: *If you're using bone-in chicken, increase the pressure cooking time by 1 or 2 minutes.*

1. Put the chicken in a zip-top bag and add 1 teaspoon of olive oil and the shawarma spice mix. Smoosh it all up together so that the chicken is evenly coated in the oil and spices.

2. At this point, you can freeze the chicken for a meal later in the week, or you could leave it in the refrigerator to marinate for up to 24 hours. (I like to make half the chicken now and freeze the other half for another meal. Clearly this "now and later" is a thing with me.)

3. Preheat the Instant Pot® by selecting Sauté and adjusting to high heat. When the inner cooking pot is hot, add the remaining 2 teaspoons of oil and heat until it is shimmering. Add the chicken in a single layer. Let it sear, then flip the pieces to the other side, about 4 minutes in total.

4. Add the onion. (Traditionally, shawarma is not cooked with onions, but we need something to add flavor to the broth and the chicken; onions not only add flavor, they also release a little water so you add less water to the Instant Pot®).

5. Pour in the water and scrape up any browned bits from the bottom of the pot.

6. Lock the lid into place. Select Manual or Pressure Cook and adjust the pressure to High. Cook for 10 minutes. When the cooking is complete, quick-release the pressure. Unlock the lid.

7. To serve, wrap the chicken in the lettuce leaves and serve with the tzatziki sauce.

Per Serving Calories: 267; Total Fat: 15g; Total Carbs: 5g; Net Carbs: 4g; Fiber: 1g; Sugar: 4g; Protein: 28g

5

Beef and Pork

Braised Beef Brisket, page 114

Easy Taco Dip

SERVES 6

A wonderful low-carb, high-fat keto taco dip with raw vegetables is perfect for game day, or anytime when you fancy a savory, satisfying snack. It's also great as a main dish with cauliflower rice or other vegetables. You eat it the way you want to, even if it's straight out of the pot with no spoon—no judging here!

1 pound 80% lean ground beef

1 cup chopped onion

4 garlic cloves, minced

1 (5-ounce) can green chiles (usually poblanos), diced

1 (10-ounce) can tomatoes with chiles, drained (such as Ro-Tel)

3 tablespoons taco seasoning

1½ cups grated sharp Cheddar cheese

PREP TIME
5 minutes

SAUTÉ
2 minutes

PRESSURE COOK/MANUAL
5 minutes high pressure

RELEASE
Natural 10 minutes, then Quick

TOTAL TIME
35 minutes

MACROS
60% Fat
13% Carbs
27% Protein

GLUTEN-FREE

SOY-FREE

UNDER 45 MINUTES

1. Preheat the Instant Pot® by selecting Sauté and adjusting to high heat. When the inner cooking pot is hot, add the ground beef, onion, and garlic. Cook until the ground beef clumps have broken up, about 2 minutes.

2. Stir in the chiles, tomatoes, and taco seasoning.

3. Lock the lid into place. Select Manual or Pressure Cook and adjust the pressure to High. Cook for 5 minutes. When the cooking is complete, let the pressure release naturally for 10 minutes, then quick-release any remaining pressure. Unlock the lid

4. Add the cheese and stir until well mixed.

Per Serving Calories: 385; Total Fat: 26g; Total Carbs: 13g; Net Carbs: 12g; Fiber: 1g; Sugar: 5g; Protein: 26g

Ground Beef Shawarma

SERVES 4

This is an easy, one-pot low-carb meal for your Instant Pot® that is also flavorful and super family-friendly. Take the few minutes to make your own Shawarma Spice Mix (page 152). You'll thank me, especially as you later use the mix to invent your own creations. Serve with a side of Tzatziki Sauce (page 154) to increase the fat content of the meal.

1 pound 80% lean ground beef

1 cup sliced onions

1 cup thickly sliced red bell peppers

2 tablespoons Shawarma Spice Mix (page 152)

1 teaspoon salt

2 cups chopped cabbage

PREP TIME
5 minutes

SAUTÉ
4 minutes

PRESSURE COOK/MANUAL
2 minutes high pressure

RELEASE
Natural 5 minutes, then Quick

TOTAL TIME
30 minutes

MACROS
65% Fat
5% Carbs
30% Protein

DAIRY-FREE

GLUTEN-FREE

SOY-FREE

5 INGREDIENTS OR LESS

UNDER 45 MINUTES

1. Preheat the Instant Pot® by selecting Sauté and adjusting to high heat. When it is hot, add the ground beef and break into chunks, sautéing, for 3 to 4 minutes. Your goal here is to break it down so that it doesn't cook as one big chunk. You're not really spending time browning it.

2. Once the beef is in smaller bits, add the onions, peppers, shawarma spice mix, and salt. Place the cabbage on top to keep it from overcooking. You won't be adding any water to this recipe, as the meat and vegetables release enough water on their own. ➤

Ground Beef Shawarma CONTINUED

3. Lock the lid into place. Select Manual or Pressure Cook and adjust the pressure to High. Cook for 2 minutes. When the cooking is complete, let the pressure release naturally for 5 minutes, then quick-release any remaining pressure. Unlock the lid.

Per Serving Calories: 358; Total Fat: 26g; Total Carbs: 7g; Net Carbs: 5g; Fiber: 2g; Sugar: 4g; Protein: 27g

TIP: *Note that the cabbage tends to cook up very soft in this dish. If you prefer cabbage with a little more crunch, cut the cabbage into large, thick slices rather than chopping it, and place it on top of the meat rather than mixing it in.*

Corned Beef and Cabbage

SERVES 8 TO 10

The trick to getting this corned beef and cabbage just right is to cook the two separately. The corned beef really needs the whole 90 minutes, and the cabbage barely even needs 90 seconds. The long cooking time for the corned beef brisket does, however, make it just melt in your mouth.

1 (2- to 3-pound) packaged corned beef brisket

½ head cabbage

1. Put the corned beef in the inner cooking pot of the Instant Pot®, fat-side up. Meat fat is a good thing.

2. The corned beef will have come with a spice packet. Empty the spice packet into the pot. Add enough water to come up a little less than halfway to covering the meat.

3. Lock the lid into place. Select Manual or Pressure Cook and adjust the pressure to High. Cook for 90 minutes. When the cooking is complete, let the pressure release naturally. Unlock the lid.

4. Carefully take out the corned beef and put it on a cutting board.

5. Meanwhile, cut the cabbage into large chunks and put them into the water left from cooking the corned beef. Lock the lid into place. Cook on high pressure for 1 minutes. When the cooking is complete, quick-release the pressure. Unlock the lid and remove the cabbage.

6. Slice the corned beef against the grain and serve with the cabbage.

Per Serving Calories: 293; Total Fat: 21g; Total Carbs: 3g; Net Carbs: 2g; Fiber: 1g; Sugar: 1g; Protein: 23g

PREP TIME
5 minutes

PRESSURE COOK/MANUAL
90 minutes, plus 2 minutes high pressure

RELEASE
Natural/Quick

TOTAL TIME
2 hours

MACROS
65% Fat
4% Carbs
31% Protein

DAIRY-FREE

GLUTEN-FREE

SOY-FREE

5 INGREDIENTS OR LESS

Ropa Vieja

SERVES 4

Preparing Cuban ropa vieja in your Instant Pot® makes an almost effortless low-carb mix of meat and vegetables. A colorful feast for the eyes as well as your tastebuds, this dish can be made with less than 10 minutes of prep time. It generates a lovely sauce to pour over mashed cauliflower or to have with a side salad for a satisfying meal.

1½ cups sliced onions

1 cup sliced bell peppers

6 garlic cloves, peeled

2 cups canned diced fire-roasted tomatoes, with their juices

1 pound beef chuck steak

1 teaspoon ground cumin

1 teaspoon salt

1 teaspoon smoked paprika

½ teaspoon ancho chili powder

½ teaspoon dried oregano

½ cup sliced pimento-stuffed olives, for garnish

PREP TIME
10 minutes

MEAT
30 minutes high pressure

RELEASE
Natural 10 minutes, then Quick

TOTAL TIME
60 minutes

MACROS
60% Fat
12% Carbs
28% Protein

DAIRY-FREE

GLUTEN-FREE

SOY-FREE

1. Put the onions, peppers, garlic, tomatoes, steak, cumin, salt, paprika, chili powder, and oregano in the inner cooking pot of the Instant Pot®.

2. Lock the lid into place. Select Meat and adjust the pressure to High. Cook for 30 minutes. When the cooking is complete, let the pressure release naturally for 10 minutes, then quick-release any remaining pressure. Unlock and remove the lid.

3. Switch the Instant Pot® to Sauté and adjust the heat to high. Bring the sauce to a boil so it stays hot.

4. Meanwhile, carefully remove the steak and cut or shred it into long slices, then add it back into the sauce.

5. Garnish with the sliced olives and serve with a side salad or over mashed cauliflower or zucchini noodles.

TIP: *Here's another "Yes I know" statement! Yes, I know ancho chili powder is not traditional in Cuban ropa vieja across all regions. But try my version before you decide it's not needed. Many of my Cuban readers rave about this recipe written just as is.*

Per Serving Calories: 342; Total Fat: 22g; Total Carbs: 12g; Net Carbs: 9g; Fiber: 3g; Sugar: 6g; Protein: 24g

Beef Curry

SERVES 4

A true curry isn't a particular dish but is anything that has been cooked with water in it. My using this ubiquitous term for this dish might put off some people who think they dislike curry. Most people who feel this way are reacting to store-bought curry powder. This dish relies instead on a variety of fresh spices that you can mix and customize to your own taste. Consider this a base curry recipe. You can easily swap the beef for chicken or lamb or pork; you need only to adjust the cooking time under pressure.

2 tomatoes, quartered

1 small onion, quartered

4 garlic cloves, chopped

½ cup fresh cilantro leaves

1 teaspoon ground cumin

½ teaspoon ground coriander

1 teaspoon Garam Masala (page 151)

½ teaspoon cayenne

1 teaspoon salt, plus more for seasoning

1 pound beef chuck roast, cut into 1-inch cubes

PREP TIME
10 minutes

PRESSURE COOK/MANUAL
20 minutes high pressure

RELEASE
Natural

TOTAL TIME
55 minutes

MACROS
61% Fat
8% Carbs
31% Protein

DAIRY-FREE

SOY-FREE

1. In a blender jar, combine the tomatoes, onion, garlic, and cilantro. (If you put the tomatoes at the bottom, they will liquefy first, and you won't have to add water.)

2. Process until all the vegetables have turned to a smooth purée. Add the cumin, coriander, garam masala, cayenne, and salt. Process for several more seconds.

3. To the inner cooking pot of the Instant Pot®, add the beef and pour the vegetable purée on top.

4. Lock the lid into place. Select Manual or Pressure Cook and adjust the pressure to High. Cook for 20 minutes. Let the pressure release naturally. Unlock and remove the lid.

5. Stir the curry. Taste and adjust, adding more salt if you like. Serve with zucchini or cucumber noodles or mashed cauliflower.

Per Serving Calories: 309; Total Fat: 21g; Total Carbs: 6g; Net Carbs: 4g; Fiber: 2g; Sugar: 2g; Protein: 24g

Spicy Basil-Beef Bowls

SERVES 6

Cook a spicy basil beef, make a quick pickled vegetable salad while it cooks, and serve a healthy, fast—and oh so satisfying—dinner. Do not skip the gochujang (see page 13 for a description of this ingredient). I've used it in several recipes in this book because there's nothing worse than buying one ingredient for one recipe—at least to me. But the flavor payoff with its complex, slightly spicy, very umami seasoning is not to be missed.

FOR THE BEEF

1 tablespoon vegetable oil

5 garlic cloves, thinly sliced

1 tablespoon julienned fresh ginger

2 dried red chiles

1 cup sliced onions

1 pound 80% lean ground beef

1 teaspoon salt

1 teaspoon freshly ground pepper

1 tablespoon gochujang, adjusted to taste

1 cup fresh basil leaves, divided

¼ cup water or chicken broth

1 tablespoon soy sauce

1 teaspoon Truvia or Swerve

2 tablespoons freshly squeezed lime juice

1 teaspoon sesame oil

FOR THE PICKLED VEGETABLES

1 carrot

1 cucumber, peeled

¼ cup white vinegar

½ teaspoon salt

½ teaspoon Truvia or Swerve

PREP TIME
5 minutes

SAUTÉ
5 minutes

PRESSURE COOK/MANUAL
4 minutes high pressure

RELEASE
Natural 5 minutes, then Quick

TOTAL TIME
35 minutes

MACROS
60% Fat
10% Carbs
30% Protein

DAIRY-FREE

UNDER 45 MINUTES

---

1. Preheat the Instant Pot® by selecting Sauté and adjusting to high heat. When the inner cooking pot is hot, add the oil and heat until it is shimmering. Add the garlic, ginger, and chiles and sauté for 30 seconds.

2. Add the onions and sauté for 1 minute.

3. Add the ground beef and break up any lumps, cooking for 3 to 4 minutes. Don't worry about cooking it through at this point; just make sure it's not going to cook as one big lump of meat. ➤

4. Add the salt, pepper, gochujang, ½ cup of basil water, soy sauce, sweetener, lime juice, and sesame oil, and stir to combine.

5. Lock the lid into place. Select Manual or Pressure Cook and adjust the pressure to High. Cook for 4 minutes. When the cooking is complete, let the pressure release naturally for 5 minutes, then quick-release any remaining pressure. Unlock the lid and stir in the remaining ½ cup of basil.

6. While the beef is cooking, pickle the vegetables for your side salad. Julienne or coarsely grate the carrots and cucumbers. Then put them in a medium bowl and mix with the vinegar, salt, and sweetener.

7. To serve, portion the basil beef into individual bowls, accompanied by the pickled salad.

Per Serving Calories: 298; Total Fat: 20g; Total Carbs: 8g; Net Carbs: 7g; Fiber: 1g; Sugar: 3g; Protein: 22g

Stroganoff

SERVES 4

Here's a dish that looks—let's admit it—terrible, but tastes creamy and wonderful. It's classic comfort food for a very good reason. It's hearty, filling, warm, and delicious. This can easily become a go-to meal during the cold winter months.

1 tablespoon unsalted butter

½ cup diced onion

1 tablespoon minced garlic

1 pound pork tips or beef stew meat

1½ cups chopped mushrooms

1 tablespoon Worcestershire sauce

1 teaspoon salt

½ to 1 teaspoon freshly ground black pepper

½ cup water

⅓ cup sour cream

¼ teaspoon xanthan gum

PREP TIME
5 minutes

SAUTÉ
5 minutes

PRESSURE COOK/MANUAL
20 minutes high pressure

RELEASE
Natural

TOTAL TIME
1 hour

MACROS
68% Fat
5% Carbs
27% Protein

GLUTEN-FREE

1. Preheat the Instant Pot® by selecting Sauté and adjusting to high heat. When the inner cooking pot is hot, add the butter and heat until it is foaming. Add the onion and garlic and stir for 4 to 5 minutes.

2. Add the beef, mushrooms, Worcestershire sauce, salt, pepper, and water.

3. Lock the lid into place. Select Manual or Pressure Cook and adjust the pressure to High. Cook for 20 minutes. When the cooking is complete, let the pressure release naturally. Unlock the lid.

4. Switch the pot to Sauté and adjust to high heat, then add the sour cream and stir.

5. Shake in the xanthan gum a little at a time and keep stirring until the sauce thickens.

6. Serve with cauliflower rice or zoodles.

Per Serving Calories: 364; Total Fat: 28g; Total Carbs: 5g; Net Carbs: 4g; Fiber: 1g; Sugar: 2g; Protein: 23g

3-2-2-1 Texas Chili

SERVES 4

Why 3-2-2-1? First, because it's super quick. Second, because that's how I remember the proportions of spices in the recipe. I know you thought this was some kind of newfangled Texas two-step dance. It's not, but you might well be doing your own dance after tasting this easy chili.

1 tablespoon vegetable oil

1 cup chopped onions

1 tablespoon minced garlic

1 pound 80% lean ground beef

1 cup canned diced fire-roasted tomatoes, with their juices

1 tablespoon chopped chipotle chiles in adobo sauce from a can

2 (6-inch) low-carb corn tortillas

3 teaspoons Mexican red chili powder (not cayenne)

2 teaspoons ground cumin

2 teaspoons salt

1 teaspoon dried oregano

½ cup water

Grated sharp Cheddar cheese, for garnish (optional)

PREP TIME
10 minutes

SAUTÉ
5 minutes

PRESSURE COOK/MANUAL
10 minutes high pressure

RELEASE
Natural 10 minutes, then Quick

TOTAL TIME
45 minutes

MACROS
69% Fat
12% Carbs
19% Protein

DAIRY-FREE

GLUTEN-FREE

SOY-FREE

TIP: *If you can't find fire-roasted tomatoes, use a can of regular tomatoes and add 1 teaspoon of liquid smoke, if available.*

1. Preheat the Instant Pot® by selecting Sauté and adjusting to high heat. When the inner cooking pot is hot, add the oil and heat until it is shimmering. Add the onions and garlic. Stir for 30 seconds and then add the ground beef. Break up the ground beef and allow it to brown slightly, cooking for 3 to 4 minutes.

2. Meanwhile, put the tomatoes, chipotle chiles with adobo sauce, and tortillas in the jar of a blender and purée until relatively smooth.

3. In a small bowl, combine the chili powder, cumin, salt, and oregano. Once the ground beef is somewhat brown (but not fully cooked), add the spice mixture and allow the spices to bloom for 30 seconds.

4. Add the tomato, chipotle, and tortilla mixture to the Instant Pot®. Use the water to wash out the blender jar and pour that into the pot.

5. Lock the lid into place. Select Manual or Pressure Cook and adjust the pressure to High. Cook for 10 minutes. When the cooking is complete, let the pressure release naturally for 10 minutes, then quick-release any remaining pressure. Unlock the lid.

6. Mix well, top with the cheese (if using), and serve.

Per Serving Calories: 433; Total Fat: 33g; Total Carbs: 13g; Net Carbs: 7g; Fiber: 6g; Sugar: 3g; Protein: 21g

Korean-Style Galbijjim

SERVES 8

This is another recipe that uses gochujang (see page 13 for a description) for maximum effect. Don't confuse this dish with Korean galbi, which is grilled. These are braised ribs. It's also important to use meaty pork ribs for this dish, not the typical thin, flanken-style Korean ribs.

2 pounds meaty short ribs

1 to 2 tablespoons gochujang

3 tablespoons soy sauce

¼ teaspoon powdered stevia

3 or 4 garlic cloves, crushed

2 teaspoons minced fresh ginger

1 tablespoon sesame oil

1 tablespoon mirin

1 teaspoon Swerve or Truvia

1 teaspoon salt

2 teaspoons freshly ground black pepper

¼ cup water

¼ teaspoon xanthan gum, if needed

PREP TIME
10 minutes, plus up to 24 hours to marinate

PRESSURE COOK/MANUAL
12 minutes high pressure

RELEASE
Natural

TOTAL TIME
50 minutes, plus time to marinate

MACROS
83% Fat
2% Carbs
15% Protein

DAIRY-FREE

1. Put the ribs into a large zip-top bag.

2. In a small bowl, whisk together the gochujang, soy sauce, stevia, garlic, ginger, sesame oil, mirin, sweetener, salt, and pepper. Pour this over the ribs and seal the bag. Smoosh the bag a bit to distribute the marinade to fully coat the ribs.

3. Marinate the ribs for at least 1 hour, or in the refrigerator for up to 24 hours.

4. Put the ribs and marinade in the inner cooking pot of the Instant Pot® along with the water.

5. Lock the lid into place. Select Manual or Pressure Cook and adjust the pressure to High. Cook for 12 minutes. When the cooking is complete, let the pressure release naturally. Unlock the lid.

6. If the sauce is too thin, turn the Instant Pot® on Sauté and adjust the heat to high. Remove the ribs to a serving platter. Once the sauce begins to boil, sprinkle in the xanthan gum, mixing well until the sauce thickens.

7. Pour the sauce over the ribs and eat!

Per Serving Calories: 467; Total Fat: 43g; Total Carbs: 3g; Net Carbs: 3g; Fiber: 0g; Sugar: 1g; Protein: 17g

Carne Guisada

SERVES 4

This is a classic Tex-Mex dish, but the traditional version requires you to stand and stir for hours. The Instant Pot® makes very quick work of this flavorful, hearty dish. It will taste just like what your abuela made—except that it didn't take all day.

½ onion, chopped

1 red bell pepper, chopped

2 tomatoes, chopped

3 garlic cloves, chopped

1 tablespoon ground cumin

½ teaspoon dried oregano

1 to 2 teaspoons salt

1 teaspoon freshly ground black pepper

1 teaspoon ancho chili powder

1 teaspoon smoked paprika

1 pound beef chuck, cut into large pieces

¾ cup water, plus 2 tablespoons

¼ teaspoon xanthan gum

PREP TIME
10 minutes

PRESSURE COOK/MANUAL
20 minutes high pressure

RELEASE
Quick

TOTAL TIME
40 minutes

MACROS
61% Fat
11% Carbs
28% Protein

DAIRY-FREE

GLUTEN-FREE

SOY-FREE

UNDER 45 MINUTES

1. In a blender, purée the onion, bell pepper, tomatoes, garlic, cumin, oregano, salt, pepper, chili powder, and paprika.

2. Put the beef pieces in the inner cooking pot of the Instant Pot®. Pour in the blended mixture.

3. Use ¾ cup of water to wash out the blender and pour that into the pot.

4. Lock the lid into place. Select Manual or Pressure Cook and adjust the pressure to High. Cook for 20 minutes. When the cooking is complete, quick-release the pressure. Unlock the lid.

5. Switch the pot to Sauté and adjust the heat to high to bring the stew to a full boil.

6. Make a slurry by mixing the xanthan gum with the remaining 2 tablespoons of water. Pour this into the boiling stew and stir until it thickens.

Per Serving Calories: 326; Total Fat: 22g; Total Carbs: 9g; Net Carbs: 7g; Fiber: 2g; Sugar: 2g; Protein: 23g

Braised Beef Brisket

SERVES 8

Having lived in Texas for 30 years, I had a tough time with not smoking my brisket. But not only is this braised-in-an-Instant-Pot® brisket an easy, savory dish you can make without heating up your entire house, it also requires little planning. The pressure cooker makes the meat very tender. It's a straightforward recipe that practically makes itself. Serve with a side of Cauliflower Rice (page 149).

1½ teaspoons salt

2 teaspoons freshly ground black pepper

2 pounds beef brisket, cut against the grain into 4 pieces

½ cup water

2 tablespoons tomato paste

2 tablespoons Worcestershire sauce

1 to 2 teaspoons liquid smoke

2 cups sliced onions

1 tablespoon prepared mustard, or to taste

½ teaspoon xanthan gum

PREP TIME
10 minutes

PRESSURE COOK/MANUAL
60 to 75 minutes high pressure

RELEASE
Natural 10 Minutes, then Quick

TOTAL TIME
1 hour 45 minutes

MACROS
68% Fat
5% Carbs
27% Protein

DAIRY-FREE

GLUTEN-FREE

1. Sprinkle the salt and pepper over the brisket pieces and let them sit while you get your other ingredients together.

2. In a small bowl, mix together the water, tomato paste, Worcestershire sauce, and liquid smoke.

3. Put the onions in the inner cooking pot of the Instant Pot®. Place the beef on top of the onions. Pour in the sauce.

4. Lock the lid into place. Select Manual or Pressure Cook and adjust the pressure to High. Cook for 60 minutes for a brisket with some chew, and 70 to 75 minutes for a more tender brisket. When the cooking is complete, let the pressure release naturally for 10 minutes, then quick-release any remaining pressure. Unlock the lid.

5. Open the pot and remove the brisket with tongs.

6. Tilting the pot slightly, use an immersion blender to blend together the onions and all the liquid in the pot. Add the mustard and stir until it is well mixed.

7. Switch the Instant Pot® to Sauté and adjust the heat to high. Add the xanthan gum, stirring well, and allow the sauce to thicken.

8. Slice the beef across the grain and serve with the sauce.

Per Serving Calories: 332; Total Fat: 25g; Total Carbs: 4g; Net Carbs: 3g; Fiber: 1g; Sugar: 2g; Protein: 21g

Turkish Kebab Gyros

SERVES 6

Now you can make homemade gyros that slice just like the ones in your favorite restaurant. Be aware that this will not be the most attractive loaf of meat you've ever seen. It will, however, be one of the tastiest you've had. If the appearance bothers you, you can either slice it right away or you can broil it in an oven to brown the top.

1 red onion, roughly chopped

6 garlic cloves

1 pound ground beef

1 pound ground pork or ground lamb

2 teaspoons ground marjoram

2 teaspoons dried rosemary

2 teaspoons dried oregano

2 teaspoons kosher salt

2 teaspoons freshly ground black pepper

1 cup Tzatziki Sauce (page 154)

PREP TIME
15 minutes

PRESSURE COOK/MANUAL
15 minutes high pressure

RELEASE
Natural

TOTAL TIME
50 minutes, plus 30 minutes to rest

MACROS
75% Fat
8% Carbs
17% Protein

GLUTEN-FREE

SOY-FREE

1. Put the onion and garlic into the bowl of a large food processor and process until they are finely chopped but not liquefied.

2. Put the ground beef and ground pork in the bowl of a sturdy stand mixer with a paddle attachment. Sprinkle the meat with the marjoram, rosemary, oregano, salt, and pepper. Add the onions and garlic. Mix the living daylights out of the meat until it's a sticky mess. Don't skip this step, or you will have a hamburger with seasonings, not a smooth gyro loaf.

3. Pour 2 cups of water into the inner cooking pot of the Instant Pot®, then place a trivet in the pot.

4. Lay out a sheet of aluminum foil, and on top of it make two meat loaf shapes out of the meat mixture, each no thicker than 4 to 5 inches.

5. Put this sheet of foil and the meat loaves on top of the trivet, leaving enough space on the sides for the steam to circulate.

6. Lock the lid into place. Select Manual or Pressure Cook and adjust the pressure to High. Cook for 15 minutes. When the cooking is complete, let the pressure release naturally. Unlock the lid.

7. When you remove the lid, don't despair at those big gray lumps. If the color bothers you, place the meat loaves under the broiler for a bit. But trust me when I tell you, no one will care about appearance once they've tasted these.

8. Take out the meat loaves and cover them with foil. Place something heavy on top to compress them. I put a cast iron skillet on top and then carefully place three cans of beans on top of the skillet.

9. Let the meat rest for 30 minutes and then cut into thin slices.

10. Serve with the tzatziki sauce and a side salad.

Per Serving Calories: 531; Total Fat: 44g; Total Carbs: 6g; Net Carbs: 6g; Fiber: 0g; Sugar: 4g; Protein: 22g

Bo Ssäm–Style Pork

SERVES 6

What is bo ssäm, *you ask? Well, traditionally, it's a pork shoulder that has been marinated and roasted slowly until it is melty and tender, then eaten wrapped in leafy greens. Or maybe it's not. Maybe it's just a term misused by famous chefs. Opinions are divided on this front, but so far there has been no division of opinion among my readers on the sheer deliciousness and ease of this dish.*

1 tablespoon vegetable oil

1 pound ground pork

1 tablespoon minced fresh ginger

1 tablespoon minced garlic

2 tablespoons gochujang (see page 13)

1 tablespoon doubanjiang (see page 13)

1 tablespoon soy sauce

½ teaspoon ground Sichuan peppercorns

1 teaspoon hot sesame oil

1 teaspoon salt

¼ cup water

1 bunch bok choy, chopped (4 to 6 cups)

PREP TIME
10 minutes

SAUTÉ
4 minutes

PRESSURE COOK/MANUAL
4 minutes high pressure

RELEASE
Quick

TOTAL TIME
30 minutes

MACROS
72% Fat
4% Carbs
24% Protein

DAIRY-FREE

UNDER 45 MINUTES

1. Preheat the Instant Pot® by selecting Sauté and adjusting to high heat. When the inner cooking pot is hot, add the oil and heat until it is shimmering. Add the ground pork, breaking up all lumps, and cook until the pork is no longer pink, 3 to 4 minutes.

2. Add the ginger, garlic, gochujang, doubanjiang, soy sauce, peppercorns, sesame oil, and salt. Stir to combine. Add the water and deglaze the pan by scraping up the browned bits from the bottom of the pot. Add the bok choy.

3. Lock the lid into place. Select Manual or Pressure Cook and adjust the pressure to High. Cook for 4 minutes. When the cooking is complete, quick-release the pressure. Unlock the lid.

4. Serve with shirataki noodles or zoodles.

Per Serving Calories: 239; Total Fat: 19g; Total Carbs: 2g; Fiber: 1g; Net Carbs: 1g; Sugar: 1g; Protein: 14g

Carne Adovada

I know you're wondering if I've lost my mind, suggesting raisins and fish sauce in carne adovada. I use those ingredients to add sweetness and umami to a dish that traditionally calls for a lot of different steps to achieve that flavor. I promise, you won't be disappointed.

¼ cup raisins

¼ cup hot water

2 pounds pork shoulder, cut into large pieces

2 teaspoons vegetable oil

1 cup chopped red onion

3 garlic cloves, chopped

1 teaspoon salt

1 teaspoon dried oregano

½ teaspoon ancho chili powder

1 chipotle chile in adobo sauce, chopped

¼ cup Mexican red chili powder (*not* cayenne)

1 tablespoon cider vinegar

¼ cup soy sauce or fish sauce

½ to ¾ cup water

½ teaspoon xanthan gum

PREP TIME
15 minutes

PRESSURE COOK/MANUAL
20 minutes high pressure

RELEASE
Natural

TOTAL TIME
60 minutes

MACROS
60% Fat
9% Carbs
31% Protein

DAIRY-FREE

1. Put the raisins in a blender jar and cover them with the hot water. Let them sit while you get everything else ready.

2. Place the pork in the inner cooking pot of the Instant Pot®.

3. In a microwave-safe bowl, combine the oil, onions, garlic, salt, oregano, ancho chili powder, chipotle chiles with sauce, and red chili powder. Microwave on high for 5 to 7 minutes, stirring once or twice.

4. Pour this mixture, the cider vinegar, and soy sauce into the blender jar with the raisins. Purée until smooth.

5. Pour this mixture over the pork.

6. Use ½ cup of water to wash out your blender jar, and pour this into the pot as well. Add another ¼ cup of water if there's still any mixture left in the blender jar.

7. Lock the lid into place. Select Manual or Pressure Cook and adjust the pressure to High. Cook for 20 minutes. When the cooking is complete, naturally release the pressure. Unlock the lid.

8. If you have too much liquid, set your pot on Sauté and adjust the heat to high. Sprinkle the xanthan gum in, stir very well, and let the sauce boil and thicken.

Per Serving Calories: 298; Total Fat: 20g; Total Carbs: 8g; Net Carbs: 6g; Fiber: 2g; Sugar: 3g; Protein: 23g

Pork Saag

SERVES 4

This recipe is a good demonstration of how you can use lactic acid–containing products, in this case half-and-half, to marinate meat. The lactic acid helps tenderize the meat, but it does so gently, meaning you can allow it to marinate for a while without overly breaking down the meat. The greens in this dish amp up an already flavorful dish that much more.

FOR THE MARINADE

⅓ cup half-and-half, plus more as needed

1 teaspoon minced garlic

1 teaspoon minced fresh ginger

½ teaspoon ground turmeric

½ teaspoon cayenne

2 teaspoons Garam Masala (page 151)

1 teaspoon salt

1 pound pork shoulder, cut into bite-size cubes

FOR FINISHING THE PORK SAAG

1 tablespoon Ghee (page 150) or peanut oil

1 tablespoon tomato paste

¾ cup water

5 ounces baby spinach, chopped

Salt, for seasoning

PREP TIME
10 minutes, plus up to 8 hours to marinate

SAUTÉ
10 minutes

PRESSURE COOK/MANUAL
10 minutes, plus 2 minutes high pressure

RELEASE
Quick then Natural

TOTAL TIME
1 hour, plus time to marinate

MACROS
64% Fat
6% Carbs
30% Protein

GLUTEN-FREE

SOY-FREE

To marinate the pork

1. In a large bowl, mix the half-and-half, garlic, ginger, turmeric, cayenne, garam masala, and salt. Add the pork and stir to coat.

2. Marinate the pork for at least 30 minutes or up to 8 hours. If you marinate for more than 30 minutes, cover and refrigerate the bowl until ready for use.

To finish the pork saag

1. Preheat the Instant Pot® by selecting Sauté and adjusting to high heat. When the inner cooking pot is hot, add the ghee and heat until it is shimmering. Add the pork along with the marinade, and the tomato paste. Cook for 5 to 10 minutes, or until the pork is lightly seared and the tomato paste has been well incorporated. Pour in the water.

2. Lock the lid into place. Select Manual or Pressure Cook and adjust the pressure to High. Cook for 10 minutes. When the cooking is complete, quick-release the pressure. Carefully remove the lid and add the spinach. Mix well to incorporate.

3. Lock the lid into place. Select Manual or Pressure Cook and adjust the pressure to High. Cook for 2 minutes. Allow the pressure to release naturally. Unlock and remove the lid.

4. Mix well and adjust the seasoning, adding more salt and half-and-half if desired.

Per Serving Calories: 335; Total Fat: 24g; Total Carbs: 7g; Net Carbs: 4g; Fiber: 3g; Sugar: 1g; Protein: 24g

TIP: This recipe can be made with any type of meat. Just use the half-and-half mixture to marinate it first.

Pork Carnitas

SERVES 4

Two kinds of chili powders and smoked paprika add a nice, smoky taste to this dish. You could just use regular chili powder and get a perfectly lovely dish as well, but the combination in this recipe adds a special depth of flavor. Please don't skip the browning in step 9. It's the difference between delicious boiled meat versus carnitas. If they're not crispy, they're not carnitas.

1 onion, sliced

4 garlic cloves, sliced

1 pound pork shoulder, cut into cubes, visible fat removed

Juice of 1 lemon

¼ teaspoon ancho chili powder

¼ teaspoon chipotle chili powder

¼ teaspoon smoked paprika

½ teaspoon dried oregano

½ teaspoon roasted cumin powder

1 to 2 teaspoons salt

1 teaspoon freshly ground black pepper

½ cup water

1 to 2 tablespoons coconut oil

½ cup sour cream

½ avocado, diced

PREP TIME
10 minutes

MEAT
35 minutes high pressure

RELEASE
Natural 10 minutes, then Quick

SAUTÉ
10 minutes

TOTAL TIME
1 hour 15 minutes

MACROS
62% Fat
9% Carbs
29% Protein

GLUTEN-FREE

SOY-FREE

1. Place the onion and garlic in the inner cooking pot of the Instant Pot® to help them release water when the meat is cooking.

2. In a large bowl, mix together the pork and lemon juice. Add the ancho chili powder, chipotle chili powder, paprika, oregano, cumin, salt, and pepper, and stir to combine.

3. Place the pork on top of the onions and garlic.

4. Pour the water into the bowl and swirl it around to get the last of the spices, then pour this onto the pork.

5. Lock the lid into place. Select Meat and adjust the pressure to High. Cook for 35 minutes. When the cooking is complete, let the pressure release naturally for 10 minutes, then quick-release any remaining pressure. Unlock the lid.

6. Remove the pork, leaving the liquid in the pot.

7. Switch the pot to Sauté and adjust the heat to high to reduce the sauce while you finish the next steps.

8. Place a cast iron skillet on the stove over medium-high heat. Once it is hot, add the oil.

9. Shred the pork, then place it in a single layer in the skillet. Let the meat brown, undisturbed, for 3 to 4 minutes.

10. When the meat is browned on the bottom, stir it and continue cooking until it's crisp in parts.

11. Once it's good and crisp, add in the sauce, a little at a time, from the pot. The skillet should be hot enough that most of it just evaporates, leaving behind the flavor. (I use almost all of my broth, small portions at a time, to flavor the meat.)

12. Serve with the sour cream and diced avocado.

Per Serving Calories: 332; Total Fat: 23g; Total Carbs: 8g; Net Carbs: 5g; Fiber: 3g; Sugar: 2g; Protein: 26g

Smoky Ribs

SERVES 4

This recipe for smoky pressure cooker ribs requires two things: a pressure cooker and a smoker. You'll get perfectly tender smoked ribs in under 2 hours, with minimal hands-on time. If you're a barbecue purist with a smoker who doesn't like sauce on your ribs, you will love this recipe, as the smoked ribs don't need it. If you're a bad planner who wants last-minute ribs, you too will love this recipe. If you don't have a smoker, a broiling option is provided here, too.

2 tablespoons barbecue rub or Mexican-spice rub (see Tip)

1 cup water

½ cup apple cider vinegar

1 rack pork baby back ribs, about 2 pounds

FOR SMOKING THE RIBS

¼ to ½ cup wood chips

FOR BROILING THE RIBS

⅓ cup prepared low-carb barbecue sauce

PREP TIME
10 minutes

PRESSURE COOK/MANUAL
20 minutes high pressure

RELEASE
Natural 10 minutes, then Quick

TOTAL TIME
50 minutes, plus up to 1 hour to smoke or 10 minutes to broil

MACROS
68% Fat
10% Carbs
22% Protein

DAIRY-FREE

5 INGREDIENTS OR LESS

1. If you're using a smoker, preheat it to 225°F. (If you do not have a smoker, skip this and broil the ribs at the end of cooking; see directions on page 128.)

2. Remove the white membrane from the bottom of the ribs. The easiest (and, really, the only effective) way to do this is to use a paper towel to grab one end of the membrane before you start to pull. With the other hand, hold the rack in place until the membrane is released.

3. Season the ribs with a rub of your choice, or use my Mexican-spice rub recipe (see Tip on page 128).

4. Pour the water and vinegar into the inner cooking pot of the Instant Pot®, then place a trivet or steamer rack in the pot.

5. Coil the ribs on the trivet so they are standing up on one end. ➤

6. Lock the lid into place. Select Manual or Pressure Cook and adjust the pressure to High. Cook for 20 minutes. When the cooking is complete, let the pressure release naturally for 10 minutes, then quick-release any remaining pressure. Unlock the lid.

7. To finish the ribs, either smoke them or place them under a broiler.

To smoke the ribs

1. If you did not preheat the smoker, do so now (see step 1 on page 126). Once preheated, put 1 cup of water in the water pan of your smoker.

2. Put the cooked ribs on the smoker rack.

3. Add the wood chips and allow the ribs to smoke for 30 minutes to 1 hour, until they are browned and acquire a smoky flavor. You do not need barbecue sauce if you are smoking the meat, as it will simply mask the beautiful smokiness of the meat.

To broil the ribs

1. Turn the oven broiler on high. Line a roasting pan with aluminum foil. Put the ribs on the foil.

2. Baste the ribs with the barbecue sauce to add flavor and keep the ribs from drying out.

3. Broil the ribs for 5 to 10 minutes, or until well-browned and cooked through.

TIP: *Here's how to make my amazing Mexican-spice rub: In a small bowl, mix together 1 tablespoon brown sugar, 1 teaspoon garlic powder, 1 teaspoon onion powder, 1 teaspoon smoked paprika, 1 teaspoon ground cumin, 1 teaspoon salt, ½ teaspoon ancho chili powder, and ½ teaspoon freshly ground black pepper. It's a great rub for these ribs, and for other beef and pork recipes.*

Per Serving Calories: 712; Total Fat: 54g; Total Carbs: 10g; Net Carbs: 10g; Fiber: 0g; Sugar: 7g; Protein: 37g

Sausages and Kale

SERVES 4

This Instant Pot® sausage and kale recipe makes a wonderful quick, low-carb supper that requires no preplanning. Use this recipe as a guideline for other vegetables of your choice. I often throw in whatever I have, such as green beans, cauliflower, or broccoli, and cook them with the sausage. If you're using those faster-cooking types of vegetables, use frozen veggies and reduce the cook time to 2 minutes.

4 smoked sausages

6 cups chopped kale

¼ cup water

1. Place the sausages in the inner cooking pot of the Instant Pot®. Top with the kale and pour in the water.

2. Lock the lid into place. Select Manual or Pressure Cook and adjust the pressure to High. Cook for 4 minutes. When the cooking is complete, let the pressure release naturally for 5 minutes, then quick-release any remaining pressure. Unlock the lid.

3. Eat and enjoy!

Per Serving Calories: 259; Total Fat: 6g; Total Carbs: 11g; Net Carbs: 9g; Fiber: 2g; Sugar: 1g; Protein: 11g

PREP TIME
5 minutes

PRESSURE COOK/MANUAL
4 minutes high pressure

RELEASE
Natural 5 minutes, then Quick

TOTAL TIME
30 minutes

MACROS
69% Fat
14% Carbs
17% Protein

DAIRY-FREE

GLUTEN-FREE

5 INGREDIENTS OR LESS

POUR AND COOK

UNDER 45 MINUTES

TIP: *Substitute any hearty greens such as collard greens and mustard greens for the kale. If you'd like to use spinach, use frozen spinach so it doesn't overcook. You can add additional vege-tables such as onions, garlic, cabbage, or green beans. Pick vegetables that won't overcook in 4 minutes (no cauliflower or broccoli, for example) and that are low-carb.*

6

Desserts

Lemon Ricotta Cheesecake, page 136

Keto Cheesecake

SERVES 6

When I first realized cream cheese was keto, and therefore cheesecake could be made keto, I was a happy girl. The first time I made sugar-free cheesecake, I was so excited that I whipped the batter a little too enthusiastically. While great exercise, it's actually bad for your cheesecake, which gets lumpy and ugly. So once you add the eggs, fold them very gently for a smooth finish. Although I'm betting you'll eat this any which way.

2 teaspoons freshly squeezed lemon juice

2 teaspoons vanilla extract or almond extract

½ cup sour cream, divided, at room temperature

½ cup Swerve, plus 2 teaspoons

8 ounces cream cheese, at room temperature

2 eggs, at room temperature

PREP TIME
15 minutes

PRESSURE COOK/MANUAL
20 minutes high pressure

RELEASE
Natural

TOTAL TIME
60 minutes, plus 6 to 8 hours to chill

MACROS
83% Fat
8% Carbs
9% Protein

GLUTEN-FREE

SOY-FREE

VEGETARIAN

1. Pour 2 cups of water into the inner cooking pot of the Instant Pot®, then place a trivet (preferably with handles) in the pot. Line the sides of a 6-inch springform pan with parchment paper.

2. In a food processor, put the lemon juice, vanilla, ¼ cup of sour cream, ½ cup of Swerve, and the cream cheese.

3. Gently but thoroughly blend all the ingredients, scraping down the sides of the bowl as needed.

4. Add the eggs and blend only as long as you need to in order to get them well incorporated, 20 to 30 seconds. Your mixture will be pourable by now.

5. Pour the mixture into the prepared pan. Cover the pan with aluminum foil and place on the trivet. (If your trivet doesn't have handles, you may wish to use a foil sling to make removing the pan easier.)

6. Lock the lid into place. Select Manual or Pressure Cook and adjust the pressure to High. Cook for 20 minutes. When the cooking is complete, let the pressure release naturally. Unlock the lid.

7. Meanwhile, in a small bowl, mix together the remaining ¼ cup of sour cream and 2 teaspoons of Swerve for the topping.

8. Take out the cheesecake and remove the foil. Spread the topping over the top. Doing this while the cheesecake is still hot helps melt the topping into the cheesecake.

9. Put the cheesecake in the refrigerator and leave it alone. Seriously. Leave it alone and let it chill for at least 6 to 8 hours. It won't taste right hot.

10. When you're ready to serve, open the sides of the pan and peel off the parchment paper. Slice and serve.

Per Serving Calories: 207; Total Fat: 19g; Total Carbs: 4g; Net Carbs: 4g; Fiber: 0g; Sugar: 2g; Protein: 5g

Pumpkin Pie Pudding

SERVES 6

This crustless pumpkin pudding pie makes a lovely low-carb dessert. It is an easy fix-and-go dessert that you can make whenever the mood strikes you. No need to wait for Thanksgiving!

Nonstick cooking spray

2 eggs

½ cup heavy (whipping) cream or almond milk (for dairy-free)

¾ cup Swerve

1 (15-ounce) can pumpkin purée

1 teaspoon pumpkin pie spice

1 teaspoon vanilla extract

FOR FINISHING

½ cup heavy (whipping) cream

PREP TIME
10 minutes

PRESSURE COOK/MANUAL
20 minutes high pressure

RELEASE
Natural 10 minutes, then Quick

TOTAL TIME
50 minutes, plus 6 to 8 hours to chill

MACROS
81% Fat
17% Carbs
2% Protein

GLUTEN-FREE

SOY-FREE

VEGETARIAN

1. Grease a 6-by-3-inch pan *extremely* well with the cooking spray, making sure it gets into all the nooks and crannies.

2. In a medium bowl, whisk the eggs. Add the cream, Swerve, pumpkin purée, pumpkin pie spice, and vanilla, and stir to mix thoroughly.

3. Pour the mixture into the prepared pan and cover it with a silicone lid or aluminum foil.

4. Pour 2 cups of water into the inner cooking pot of the Instant Pot®, then place a trivet in the pot. Place the covered pan on the trivet.

5. Lock the lid into place. Select Manual or Pressure Cook and adjust the pressure to High. Cook for 20 minutes. When the cooking is complete, let the pressure release naturally for 10 minutes, then quick-release any remaining pressure. Unlock the lid.

6. Remove the pan and place it in the refrigerator. Chill for 6 to 8 hours.

7. When ready to serve, finish by making the whipped cream. Using a hand mixer, beat the heavy cream until it forms soft peaks. Do not overbeat and turn it to butter. Serve each pudding with a dollop of whipped cream.

Per Serving Calories: 188; Total Fat: 17g; Total Carbs: 8g; Net Carbs: 6g; Fiber: 2g; Sugar: 3g; Protein: 4g

Lemon Ricotta Cheesecake

SERVES 6

I'm not sure which part of this recipe sounds best to me—the lemon, the ricotta, or the cheesecake? This is a delicious low-carb cheesecake. The lemon zest imparts a little extra zing of flavor. You won't miss the crust when you taste this creamy, tangy concoction.

Unsalted butter or vegetable oil, for greasing the pan

8 ounces cream cheese, at room temperature

¼ cup Swerve, plus 1 teaspoon, and more as needed

⅓ cup full-fat or part-skim ricotta cheese, at room temperature

Zest of 1 lemon

Juice of 1 lemon

½ teaspoon lemon extract

2 eggs, at room temperature

2 tablespoons sour cream

PREP TIME
10 minutes

PRESSURE COOK/MANUAL
30 minutes high pressure

RELEASE
Natural

TOTAL TIME
1 hour 10 minutes, plus 6 to 8 hours to chill

MACROS
71% Fat
18% Carbs
11% Protein

GLUTEN-FREE

SOY-FREE

VEGETARIAN

1. Grease a 6-inch springform pan extremely well. I find this easiest to do with a silicone basting brush so I can get into all the nooks and crannies. Alternatively, line the sides of the pan with parchment paper.

2. In the bowl of a stand mixer, beat the cream cheese, ¼ cup of Swerve, the ricotta, lemon zest, lemon juice, and lemon extract on high speed until you get a smooth mixture with no lumps.

3. Taste to ensure the sweetness is to your liking and adjust if needed.

4. Add the eggs, reduce the speed to low and gently blend until the eggs are just incorporated. Overbeating at this stage will result in a cracked crust.

5. Pour the mixture into the prepared pan and cover with aluminum foil or a silicone lid.

6. Pour 2 cups of water into the inner cooking pot of the Instant Pot®, then place a trivet in the pot. Place the covered pan on the trivet.

7. Lock the lid into place. Select Manual or Pressure Cook and adjust the pressure to High. Cook for 30 minutes. When the cooking is complete, let the pressure release naturally. Unlock the lid.

8. Carefully remove the pan from the pot, and remove the foil.

9. In a small bowl, mix together the sour cream and remaining 1 teaspoon of Swerve and spread this over the top of the warm cake.

10. Refrigerate the cheesecake for 6 to 8 hours. Do not be in a hurry! The cheesecake needs every bit of this time to be its best.

Per Serving Calories: 217; Total Fat: 17g; Total Carbs: 10g; Net Carbs: 10g; Fiber: 0g; Sugar: 2g; Protein: 6g

Thai Coconut Pandan Custard

SERVES 4

If you've never tried pandan *before, you're in for a treat. People compare it to vanilla, but really there's no comparison—and I say this as someone who adores vanilla. I don't like buying one ingredient for one dish, but for this one, it's worth making an exception.*

Nonstick cooking spray

1 cup unsweetened coconut milk

3 eggs

⅓ cup Swerve

3 to 4 drops pandan extract, or use vanilla extract if you must

1. Grease a 6-inch heatproof bowl with the cooking spray.

2. In a large bowl, whisk together the coconut milk, eggs, Swerve, and pandan extract. Pour the mixture into the prepared bowl and cover it with aluminum foil.

3. Pour 2 cups of water into the inner cooking pot of the Instant Pot®, then place a trivet in the pot. Place the bowl on the trivet.

4. Lock the lid into place. Select Manual or Pressure Cook and adjust the pressure to High. Cook for 30 minutes. When the cooking is complete, let the pressure release naturally. Unlock the lid.

5. Remove the bowl from the pot and remove the foil. A knife inserted into the custard should come out clean. Cool in the refrigerator for 6 to 8 hours, or until the custard is set.

Per Serving Calories: 202; Total Fat: 18g; Total Carbs: 4g; Net Carbs: 3g; Fiber: 1g; Sugar: 2g; Protein: 6g

PREP TIME
10 minutes

PRESSURE COOK/MANUAL
30 minutes high pressure

RELEASE
Natural

TOTAL TIME
1 hour 5 minutes, plus 6 to 8 hours to chill

MACROS
80% Fat
7% Carbs
13% Protein

DAIRY-FREE

GLUTEN-FREE

SOY-FREE

VEGETARIAN

5 INGREDIENTS OR LESS

TIP: *Pandan is an herbaceous tropical plant that grows in Southeast-Asia. Pandan extract has a sweet, floral aroma and flavor. It can be found in many Asian markets or online.*

Indian Zucchini Kheer

SERVES 4

This super-easy Indian zucchini kheer is made in minutes in your Instant Pot®. It's a great way to use up all that summer zucchini in a sweet, exotic dessert. You could reduce the carb count even more by substituting almond milk for the evaporated milk, although your kheer might be a little less thick. The flavor is still there, of course.

2 cups shredded zucchini

5 ounces evaporated milk

5 ounces half-and-half

¼ cup Swerve

½ teaspoon ground cardamom

1. Put the zucchini, evaporated milk, half-and-half, and Swerve in the inner cooking pot of the Instant Pot®.

2. Lock the lid into place. Select Manual or Pressure Cook and adjust the pressure to High. Cook for 10 minutes. When the cooking is complete, let the pressure release naturally for 10 minutes, then quick-release any remaining pressure. Unlock the lid.

3. Add the ground cardamom and stir to mix in.

4. Serve hot or allow it to chill before serving.

Per Serving Calories: 111; Total Fat: 7g; Total Carbs: 8g; Net Carbs: 7g; Fiber: 1g; Sugar: 5g; Protein: 4g

PREP TIME
5 minutes

PRESSURE COOK/MANUAL
10 minutes high pressure

RELEASE
Natural 10 minutes, then Quick

TOTAL TIME
35 minutes

MACROS
58% Fat
29% Carbs
13% Protein

GLUTEN-FREE

SOY-FREE

VEGETARIAN

5 INGREDIENTS OR LESS

POUR AND COOK

UNDER 45 MINUTES

Coconut-Almond Cake

SERVES 8

I like making recipes with almond flour so I don't have to stock specialty baking supplies. Almond flour bakes up really toasty, so it works for both baking and pressure cooking.

Nonstick cooking spray

1 cup almond flour

½ cup unsweetened shredded coconut

⅓ cup Swerve

1 teaspoon baking powder

1 teaspoon apple pie spice

2 eggs, lightly whisked

¼ cup unsalted butter, melted

½ cup heavy (whipping) cream

1. Grease a 6-inch round cake pan with the cooking spray.

2. In a medium bowl, mix together the almond flour, coconut, Swerve, baking powder, and apple pie spice.

3. Add the eggs, then the butter, then the cream, mixing well after each addition.

4. Pour the batter into the pan and cover with aluminum foil.

5. Pour 2 cups of water into the inner cooking pot of the Instant Pot®, then place a trivet in the pot. Place the pan on the trivet.

6. Lock the lid into place. Select Manual or Pressure Cook and adjust the pressure to High. Cook for 40 minutes. When the cooking is complete, let the pressure release naturally for 10 minutes, then quick-release any remaining pressure. Unlock the lid.

7. Carefully take out the pan and let it cool for 15 to 20 minutes. Invert the cake onto a plate. Sprinkle with shredded coconut, almond slices, or powdered sweetener, if desired, and serve.

PREP TIME
10 minutes

PRESSURE COOK/MANUAL
40 minutes high pressure

RELEASE
Natural 10 minutes, then Quick

TOTAL TIME
50 minutes, plus 20 minutes to cool

MACROS
74% Fat
21% Carbs
5% Protein

GLUTEN-FREE

SOY-FREE

VEGETARIAN

Per Serving Calories: 231; Total Fat: 19g; Total Carbs: 12g; Net Carbs: 10g; Fiber: 2g; Sugar: 1g; Protein: 3g

Dark Chocolate Cake

SERVES 6

There are some great recipes in this chapter, but this one might be your best keto dessert recipe ever. Deep chocolate flavor—need I say more? This is without a doubt my personal favorite. I love that it tastes so much more sinful than it really is, but I also love how easy it is to put together. A little too easy, really!

1 cup almond flour

⅔ cup Swerve

¼ cup unsweetened cocoa powder

¼ cup chopped walnuts

1 teaspoon baking powder

3 eggs

⅓ cup heavy (whipping) cream

¼ cup coconut oil

Nonstick cooking spray

PREP TIME
10 minutes

PRESSURE COOK/MANUAL
20 minutes high pressure

RELEASE
Natural 10 minutes, then Quick

TOTAL TIME
50 minutes

MACROS
80% Fat
7% Carbs
13% Protein

GLUTEN-FREE

SOY-FREE

VEGETARIAN

1. Put the flour, Swerve, cocoa powder, walnuts, baking powder, eggs, cream, and coconut oil in a large bowl. Using a hand mixer on high speed, combine the ingredients until the mixture is well incorporated and looks fluffy. This will keep the cake from being too dense.

2. With the cooking spray, grease a heatproof pan, such as a 3-cup Bundt pan, that fits inside your Instant Pot®. Pour the cake batter into the pan and cover with aluminum foil.

3. Pour 2 cups of water into the inner cooking pot of the Instant Pot®, then place a trivet in the pot. Place the pan on the trivet.

4. Lock the lid into place. Select Manual or Pressure Cook and adjust the pressure to High. Cook for 20 minutes. When the cooking is complete, let the pressure release naturally for 10 minutes, then quick-release any remaining pressure.

5. Carefully take out the pan and let it cool for 15 to 20 minutes. Invert the cake onto a plate. It can be served hot or at room temperature. Serve with a dollop of whipped cream, if desired.

Per Serving Calories: 225; Total Fat: 20g; Total Carbs: 4g; Net Carbs: 2g; Fiber: 2g; Sugar: 0g; Protein: 5g

Almond-Carrot Cake

SERVES 8

This is one of my favorite ever cakes. I'll take this cake over a regular, sugared cake anytime. Since it's so easy to make (and eat!), I whip it up quite frequently when we need a little sweet treat. If you're worried about carrots on keto, check out the macros—carbs are kept low by using only a small quantity of carrots.

Nonstick cooking spray

3 eggs

1 cup almond flour

⅔ cup Swerve

1 teaspoon baking powder

1½ teaspoons apple pie spice

¼ cup coconut oil

½ cup heavy (whipping) cream

1 cup grated carrots

½ cup walnuts, chopped

PREP TIME
10 minutes

CAKE OR PRESSURE
Cook/Manual:
40 minutes high pressure

RELEASE
Natural 10 minutes, then Quick

TOTAL TIME
1 hour 10 minutes

MACROS
77% Fat
12% Carbs
11% Protein

GLUTEN-FREE

SOY-FREE

VEGETARIAN

1. Grease a 6-inch cake pan with the cooking spray.

2. Put the eggs, almond flour, Swerve, baking powder, apple pie spice, oil, cream, carrots, and walnuts in a large bowl. Using a hand mixer on high speed, mix until the ingredients are well incorporated and the batter looks fluffy. This will keep the cake from being dense.

3. Pour the batter into the pan and cover with aluminum foil.

4. Pour 2 cups of water into the inner cooking pot of the Instant Pot®, then place a trivet in the pot. Place the cake pan on the trivet.

5. Lock the lid into place. Select Cake or Manual or Pressure Cook, and adjust the pressure to High. Cook for 40 minutes. When the cooking is complete, let the pressure release naturally for 10 minutes, then quick-release any remaining pressure. Unlock the lid.

6. Remove the cake from the pot. Let it cool to room temperature, then invert the cake onto a plate. Ice the cake with a frosting of your choice, or serve plain.

Per Serving Calories: 198; Total Fat: 17g; Total Carbs: 5g; Net Carbs: 3g; Fiber: 2g; Sugar: 1g; Protein: 4g

TIP: *Feel free to substitute zucchini for the carrots in this recipe to further reduce carbs.*

7

Kitchen Staples

(left) Soft- and Hard-Boiled Eggs, page 148

Soft- and Hard-Boiled Eggs

MAKES 6 EGGS

The ability to make boiled eggs that peel very easily is definitely one of the most touted features of the Instant Pot®. There are as many ways to make eggs as there are people, so I will tell you from experience, there's no one foolproof , always-works way of making eggs that don't turn green around the yolks. Experiment and see what works most often for you. The eggs pictured on page 146 were cooked for 4 minutes at high pressure.

6 eggs   2 cups water, for steaming

1. In the inner cooking pot of the Instant Pot®, place a trivet or steamer basket. Pour in the water. Lay the eggs on the trivet or basket.

2. Lock the lid into place. Select Steam and adjust the pressure to High. Set the timer based on how you want your eggs to be cooked:

- *Soft-boiled, runny yolks:* 2 minutes
- *Hard-boiled, fully-set but soft yolks:* 4 minutes
- *Soft-boiled, half-set yolks:* 3 minutes
- *Hard-boiled, fully-set hard yolks:* 5 minutes

3. While the eggs cook, make an ice bath by filling a medium-size bowl halfway with cold water, then add a handful of ice cubes. Set aside.

4. After cooking, quickly release the pressure. Unlock and remove the lid, and use tongs to transfer the eggs to the ice bath.

5. After about 5 minutes, drain the water. Peel and enjoy the eggs or store them in their shells in the refrigerator until ready to eat.

Per Serving (1 egg) Calories: 71; Total Fat: 5g; Total Carbs: 0g; Net Carbs: 0g; Fiber: 0g; Sugar: 0g; Protein: 6g

PRESSURE COOK/MANUAL
2 to 5 minutes high pressure

RELEASE
Quick

TOTAL TIME
12 to 15 minutes

MACROS
63% Fat
2% Carbs
35% Protein

DAIRY-FREE

GLUTEN-FREE

SOY-FREE

VEGETARIAN

5 INGREDIENTS OR LESS

POUR AND COOK

UNDER 45 MINUTES

Cauliflower Rice

MAKES 6 CUPS

It's almost impossible to follow keto without learning to love cauliflower rice. To be honest, it doesn't taste exactly like rice, but it can taste quite good, especially if you flavor it. It is also a great accompaniment to dishes such as curries and thicker stews.

6 cups cauliflower florets, divided

Water to cover the florets (about 6 cups)

1. Put 3 cups of cauliflower florets in a blender with plenty of water, and pulse a few times until the cauliflower is all chopped up. Do not overdo the pulsing and do not get distracted, or you will end up with soup.

2. Place a wire strainer in a large bowl. Pour the cauliflower florets and water into the strainer.

3. Meanwhile, repeat the pulsing and draining with the remaining 3 cups of cauliflower florets.

4. Once the water is drained, you are ready either to cook the cauliflower or save it for later. (If you are saving for later, it will last for 3 to 4 days in the refrigerator.)

5. To cook the cauliflower, steam it in the microwave for 3 minutes or on the stove top for 5 minutes. Your goal is to cook it just long enough to get the rice al dente. Cauliflower overcooks very easily, and it continues to cook after you take it off the stove, so, if in doubt, undercook slightly.

Per Serving (1 cup) Calories: 34; Total Fat: 0g; Total Carbs: 8g; Net Carbs: 4g; Fiber: 4g; Sugar: 4g; Protein: 2g

PREP TIME
5 minutes

COOK TIME
3 to 5 minutes

TOTAL TIME
8 to 10 minutes

MACROS
3% Fat
78% Carbs
19% Protein

DAIRY-FREE

GLUTEN-FREE

SOY-FREE

VEGAN

5 INGREDIENTS OR LESS

UNDER 45 MINUTES

TIP: *Try these variations:*
- *Cook with plain chicken broth.*
- *Add ghee and salt.*
- *Add chopped cilantro and fresh lime juice.*
- *Sauté onions and bacon until the bacon is crisp, and add the cauliflower.*
- *Sauté your favorite spice blend in butter, and add the cauliflower rice.*
- *Take your favorite meat and rice recipe, substitute cooked ground meat, and cook with the riced cauliflower.*

Ghee

MAKES 1½ CUPS

One of the things we all love about keto is that fats not only fill us up—they also taste wonderful. It's hard to find something I like better than ghee to add fat and flavor to a meal—well, maybe apart from bacon. Making ghee takes 20 minutes, but it lasts for months and can be used in both sweet and savory recipes. Note that there are several Instant Pot® ghee recipes on the Internet, but they either use the Slow Cook function or use the Instant Pot® on Sauté as a pan. I do mine on the stove top for two reasons: It's faster, and the pot I have to clean is smaller than the one in the Instant Pot®.

1 pound unsalted butter

1. In a heavy-bottomed pan, heat the butter over low heat. Let the butter melt and foam. Don't mess with this too much; it's really not necessary to stir or fuss with it.

2. As the butter stops foaming, the milk solids will start turning brown and settle on the bottom of the pan. The browning is necessary to create the authentic, slightly nutty taste of the ghee.

3. When the butter is well browned, remove the pan from the heat, let the ghee cool a little, and pour it through a fine-mesh strainer or cheesecloth into an airtight jar. Ghee doesn't require refrigeration and is shelf stable, so leave it on your counter for easy access when cooking.

Per Serving (1 tablespoon) Calories: 112; Total Fat: 12g; Total Carbs: 0g; Net Carbs: 0g; Fiber: 0g; Sugar: 0g; Protein: 0g

PREP TIME
2 minutes

COOK TIME
10 minutes

TOTAL TIME
12 minutes

MACROS
100% Fat
0% Carbs
0% Protein

GLUTEN-FREE

SOY-FREE

VEGETARIAN

5 INGREDIENTS OR LESS

UNDER 45 MINUTES

Garam Masala

You don't want to incite my wrath about the importance of making garam masala. You would be better advised to take my word for it: Making your own spice blend, from whole spices, will elevate your cooking like nothing else can. Take the few minutes needed to make this blend, and I promise, you will never use store-bought garam masala again.

2 tablespoons coriander seeds

1 teaspoon cumin seeds

½ teaspoon whole cloves

½ teaspoon cardamom seeds from green or white pods

2 dried bay leaves

3 dried red chiles or ½ teaspoon cayenne or red chile flakes

1 (2-inch) piece cinnamon stick

PREP TIME
5 minutes

MACROS
3% Fat
97% Carbs
0% Protein

DAIRY-FREE

GLUTEN-FREE

SOY-FREE

VEGAN

UNDER 45 MINUTES

1. In a clean coffee or spice grinder, combine all the ingredients. Grind until the spices form a medium-fine powder. Stop the grinder several times and shake it so all the seeds and bits get under the blades and grind evenly.

2. Unplug the grinder. Holding the lid in place, turn the spice grinder upside down and shake the spice mixture into the lid. Pour the garam masala into a small jar with an airtight lid. Store in a cool, dry place for up to 3 to 4 weeks.

Per Serving (1 teaspoon) Calories: 2; Total Fat: 0g; Total Carbs: 1g; Net Carbs: 1g; Fiber: 0g; Sugar: 0g; Protein: 0g

Shawarma Spice Mix

MAKES ABOUT 3 TABLESPOONS

Make your own shawarma spice mix and use it with a variety of meats, including chicken, beef, lamb, and ground beef, or even use it with vegetables like green beans. Trust me, make lots of this: Triple or even quadruple the recipe so you have it on hand for when you decide the flavors of shawarma are just what you are looking for.

2 teaspoons dried oregano

1 teaspoon ground cinnamon

½ teaspoon ground allspice

½ teaspoon cayenne

1 teaspoon ground cumin

1 teaspoon ground coriander

1 teaspoon salt

1. Place all the ingredients in a jar with an airtight lid. Shake to combine. Store in a cool, dark place. Give the jar a shake or two before using.

Per Serving (1 teaspoon) Calories: 3; Total Fat: 0g; Total Carbs: 1g; Net Carbs: 1g; Fiber: 0g; Sugar: 0g; Protein: 0g

PREP TIME
5 minutes

MACROS
1% Fat
98% Carbs
1% Protein

DAIRY-FREE

GLUTEN-FREE

SOY-FREE

VEGAN

UNDER 45 MINUTES

Best-Ever Savory Thyme Dip

MAKES ABOUT ⅔ CUP

This great keto savory dip goes just as well with vegetables as it does with grilled meats. I know, I know, you're looking at this wondering how I can even call this a recipe and how it could possibly taste good with hardly anything in it. But it's literally one of the best dressings I've ever made. Try it, and your doubts will melt away.

½ cup mayonnaise

2 tablespoons minced fresh thyme

2 tablespoons minced red onion

1½ teaspoons freshly squeezed lemon juice

1. In a small bowl, mix the mayonnaise, thyme, onion, and lemon juice together. Cover the bowl with plastic wrap and let the mixture rest in the refrigerator for 2 hours before serving.

2. This dip will keep for 3 to 5 days in your refrigerator.

Per Serving (2 tablespoons) Calories: 87; Total Fat: 7g; Total Carbs: 6g; Net Carbs: 6g; Fiber: 0g; Sugar: 2g; Protein: 0g

PREP TIME
5 minutes

TOTAL TIME
5 minutes, plus 2 hours to chill

MACROS
72% Fat
28% Carbs
0% Protein

DAIRY-FREE

GLUTEN-FREE

VEGETARIAN

5 INGREDIENTS OR LESS

TIP: *The dip goes really well with steamed shrimp, fresh garden tomatoes, or with grilled chicken or steak.*

Tzatziki Sauce

This is another example of a simple but delicious recipe where you basically throw things together in a bowl and put it on the dinner table. It's hard to see how five little ingredients can produce so much flavor, but somehow they do, and it all works beautifully. Note that while traditional tzatziki is made with Greek yogurt, this recipe uses sour cream to add additional fat to your diet.

1 large cucumber, peeled and grated (about 2 cups)

1 cup sour cream

2 or 3 garlic cloves, minced

1 tablespoon tahini

Dash freshly squeezed lemon juice

Salt, for seasoning

Chopped parsley, for garnish (optional)

1. In a medium bowl, stir together the cucumber, sour cream, garlic, tahini, lemon juice, and salt. Garnish the sauce with parsley (if using).

Per Serving (¼ cup) Calories: 56; Total Fat: 4g; Total Carbs: 3g; Net Carbs: 3g; Fiber: 0g; Sugar: 3g; Protein: 2g

PREP TIME
10 minutes

MACROS
64% Fat
19% Carbs
17% Protein

GLUTEN-FREE

SOY-FREE

VEGETARIAN

5 INGREDIENTS OR LESS

UNDER 45 MINUTES

TIP: *This sauce has many uses. It's particularly good with the Turkish Kebab Gyros (page 116) and Chicken Shawarma (page 94).*

Mustard Dressing

MAKES ABOUT 2 CUPS

The wonderful thing about this dressing—apart from the taste, of course—is just how versatile it is. Use it with salads, grilled meats, as a dip, or over steamed vegetables for a lovely flavor. The thing I love about it the most, however, is that it just melts onto veggies, creating a wonderful, glaze-like finish. It keeps in a covered container in the refrigerator for a week or two.

1 cup extra-virgin olive oil

¾ cup apple cider vinegar

¼ cup Dijon mustard or other prepared mustard

1 tablespoon soy sauce

1 tablespoon Truvia

4 garlic cloves, minced

1 teaspoon salt

1 teaspoon freshly ground black pepper

PREP TIME
5 minutes

MACROS
97% Fat
3% Carbs
0% Protein

DAIRY-FREE

VEGETARIAN

UNDER 45 MINUTES

1. Place the ingredients in a powerful blender and blend for 1 minute until well emulsified.

2. Store in an airtight jar in the refrigerator for up to 2 weeks, shaking the jar before each use.

Per Serving (2 tablespoons) Calories: 121; Total Fat: 13g; Total Carbs: 1g; Net Carbs: 1g; Fiber: 0g; Sugar: 1g; Protein: 0g

Easy Asian Peanut Dressing

MAKES ABOUT ¾ CUP

This easy peanut dressing is fast, savory, and delicious. Throw things into your blender, give it a whirl, and eat. I use this as a salad dressing, but it's equally good as a dip for veggies, especially cucumber spears. Yum!

⅓ cup creamy peanut butter

¼ cup hot water

2 tablespoons soy sauce

2 tablespoons white vinegar

Juice of 1 lime

1 teaspoon minced fresh ginger

1 teaspoon minced garlic

1 teaspoon freshly ground black pepper

1. Put the peanut butter, water, soy sauce, vinegar, lime juice, ginger, garlic, and pepper into a powerful blender and blend for 1 minute, until well emulsified.

2. Store in an airtight jar in the refrigerator for up to 1 week.

Per Serving (2 tablespoons) Calories: 99; Total Fat: 7g; Total Carbs: 5g; Net Carbs: 1g; Fiber: 1g; Sugar: 2g; Protein: 4g

PREP TIME
5 minutes

MACROS
64% Fat
16% Carbs
20% Protein

DAIRY-FREE

VEGAN

UNDER 45 MINUTES

TIP: *Serve with vegetables, leftover cooked chicken, or as a dressing on your favorite salad.*

Creamy Cilantro-Jalapeño Dressing

MAKES ABOUT 1 CUP

This dressing looks simple, but the taste is dynamite. I won't be surprised if you have trouble keeping yourself from just sipping this dressing. That should tell you how good it is.

½ cup chopped fresh cilantro

½ cup sour cream or Greek yogurt

½ to 1 jalapeño (depending on how spicy you want the dressing)

6 garlic cloves

1 teaspoon salt

¼ cup water

1. Put the cilantro, sour cream, jalapeño, garlic, salt, and water into a powerful blender and blend for 1 minute, until well emulsified.

2. Store in an airtight jar in the refrigerator for up to 1 week.

Per Serving (2 tablespoons) Calories: 39; Total Fat: 3g; Total Carbs: 2g; Net Carbs: 2g; Fiber: 0g; Sugar: 0g; Protein: 1g

PREP TIME
10 minutes

MACROS
69% Fat
21% Carbs
10% Protein

GLUTEN-FREE

SOY-FREE

VEGETARIAN

5 INGREDIENTS OR LESS

UNDER 45 MINUTES

TIP: *This dressing is wonderful served with grilled meats of any kind, it's awesome drizzled over brisket tacos, and it's amazing with steamed vegetables. It also perks up a regular salad.*

INSTANT POT® FAQS

I often post Instant Pot® recipes on my blog, and I always get lots of comments and feedback, which I love. While many people quickly master a few recipes, many wish to do even more with the appliance. Even though it's my priority to create easy, simple recipes, I still want those recipes to help you explore and enjoy your appliance, as well as expand your palate. Here are some of the questions I get most often, and my answers to help you on your keto cooking journey.

WHEN SHOULD I USE NATURAL RELEASE VERSUS QUICK RELEASE?

Many of the recipes call for a combination of both. I prefer to use natural release for 10 minutes and then quick-release the remaining pressure. It is actually a myth that all meats require natural release or else they will be tough.

There are two situations where I use quick release:

- Many vegetables and seafoods such as fish or shrimp require a short cooking time. Allowing them to release pressure naturally results in an overcooked dish.

- Quick release is often used when you plan to add items to a dish halfway through cooking. This style of cooking in stages can be quite useful when you're making a beef stew, for example, where the meat takes longer to cook than the vegetables you might be adding during a second cooking cycle. In this case, you release pressure quickly after cooking the meat, add the vegetables, and then release pressure quickly at the end to avoid overcooking.

(*left*) Creamy Cilantro-Jalapeño Dressing, page 157

CAN I DOUBLE THE RECIPE,
AND IF SO, DO I NEED TO ADD MORE TIME?

You can certainly vary the serving sizes for any of these recipes without increasing the cooking time—cooking time under pressure, that is. But the fuller your pot, the longer it will take to come to pressure. Once under pressure, however, eight chicken thighs will cook as quickly as four thighs. So allow for longer total cooking times, but you don't need to increase time under pressure.

Since this question is asked so often, let me use an example. Let's say you're making tea and you need to let the tea steep for 5 minutes. If you're making 4 cups of tea, your 4 cups of water will come to a boil very quickly and you can then steep for 5 minutes for the tea to brew.

If you're making 10 cups of tea, the water for the tea will take longer to boil, but you still need to steep the tea for 5 minutes once the water has boiled, right?

It's the same with pressure cooking. When you double a recipe, the time it takes for the pot to come to pressure increases (boiling 4 cups of water versus 10 cups of water). But the time it takes for the item to cook under pressure (5 minutes to steep the tea), stays the same.

HOW MUCH LIQUID DO I NEED FOR EVERY RECIPE?

We've all been told that the Instant Pot® needs at least 1 cup of liquid before it can come to pressure. Yet many recipes in this book call for no added water. How is that possible? The answer is that you do need water for the Instant Pot® to come to pressure. But I prefer to get that water from the meat and vegetables directly. Most meats and vegetables tend to release a lot of water as they cook. This flavorful broth seasons the dish better than tap water can. It also keeps you from having to boil away the excess water at the end, which can result in an overcooked dish. Pressure cooking imparts a better taste because it keeps your meat from being boiled as it cooks. Using the Sauté setting to boil excess water defeats that purpose.

HOW FULL CAN I FILL THE POT? TO THE MAX LINE?

This is a commonly asked question, with an answer that is just as commonly ignored. Your inner cooking pot should not be more than two-thirds full of liquids or meats. If you're cooking foods that foam, such as beans or pasta (which you are not likely to be cooking on keto!), it should not be more than half full. This is an important safety consideration that should be heeded. Not only will the Instant Pot® shut itself off if you overfill, thus delaying your dinner, but you also do not want the contents to overheat and boil over.

The only time when it is acceptable to have anything that is over the full line in your Instant Pot® is when you are doing pot-in-pot cooking, and it is the inserted pot that exceeds the line. Placing a pot over a trivet to cook the vegetables along with your meat is one such instance.

CAN I SUBSTITUTE PROTEINS IN THE RECIPES?

It's very easy to customize many of the dishes by using the animal protein of your choice. Different meats have varying amounts of connective tissue and fat, which means that they cook at different rates. Substituting one for another is usually possible—just with a shorter or longer cooking time. The Instant Pot® Pressure Cooking Time Charts (page 162) show recommended times for different types of meats. Feel free to experiment by switching out meats to suit your tastes while adding variety to your diet and your cooking repertoire.

INSTANT POT® PRESSURE COOKING TIME CHARTS

The following charts provide approximate times for a variety of foods. To begin, you may want to cook for a minute or two less than the times listed; you can always simmer foods on Sauté to finish cooking.

Keep in mind that these times are for the foods partially submerged in water (or broth) or steamed, and for the foods cooked alone. The cooking times for the same foods when they are part of a recipe may differ because of additional ingredients or cooking liquids, or a different release method than the one listed here.

For any foods labeled with "Natural" release, allow at least 10 minutes natural pressure release before quick-releasing any remaining pressure.

MEAT

Except as noted, these times are for braised meats—that is, meats that are seared, then partially submerged in liquid and pressure cooked.

	MINUTES UNDER PRESSURE	PRESSURE	RELEASE
BEEF, SHOULDER (CHUCK) ROAST (2 LB.)	35	High	Natural
BEEF, SHOULDER (CHUCK), CUT INTO 2-INCH CHUNKS	20	High	Natural for 10 minutes
BEEF, BONE-IN SHORT RIBS	25	High	Natural
BEEF, FLAT IRON STEAK, CUT INTO ½-INCH STRIPS	1	Low	Quick
BEEF, SIRLOIN STEAK, CUT INTO ½-INCH STRIPS	1	Low	Quick
LAMB, SHOULDER, CUT INTO 2-INCH CHUNKS	20	High	Natural
LAMB, SHANKS	40	High	Natural
PORK, SHOULDER ROAST (2 LB.)	30	High	Natural
PORK, SHOULDER, CUT INTO 2-INCH CHUNKS	20	High	Natural
PORK, TENDERLOIN	4	Low	Quick
PORK, BACK RIBS (STEAMED)	25	High	Quick
PORK, SPARE RIBS (STEAMED)	20	High	Quick
PORK, SMOKED SAUSAGE, CUT INTO ½-INCH SLICES	20	High	Quick

POULTRY

Except as noted, these times are for braised poultry—that is, partially submerged in liquid.

	MINUTES UNDER PRESSURE	PRESSURE	RELEASE
CHICKEN BREAST, BONE-IN (STEAMED)	8	Low	Natural for 5 minutes
CHICKEN BREAST, BONELESS (STEAMED)	5	Low	Natural for 8 minutes
CHICKEN THIGH, BONE-IN	12	High	Natural for 10 minutes
CHICKEN THIGH, BONELESS	8	High	Natural for 10 minutes
CHICKEN THIGH, BONELESS, CUT INTO 1- TO 2-INCH PIECES	5	High	Quick
CHICKEN, WHOLE (SEARED ON ALL SIDES)	12–14	Low	Natural for 8 minutes
DUCK QUARTERS, BONE-IN	35	High	Quick
TURKEY BREAST, TENDERLOIN (12 OZ.) (STEAMED)	5	Low	Natural for 8 minutes
TURKEY THIGH, BONE-IN	30	High	Natural

SEAFOOD

All times are for steamed fish and shellfish.

	MINUTES UNDER PRESSURE	PRESSURE	RELEASE
CLAMS	2	High	Quick
MUSSELS	1	High	Quick
SALMON, FRESH (1-INCH THICK)	5	Low	Quick
HALIBUT, FRESH (1-INCH THICK)	3	High	Quick
TILAPIA OR COD, FRESH	1	Low	Quick
TILAPIA OR COD, FROZEN	3	Low	Quick
LARGE SHRIMP, FROZEN	2	Low	Quick

VEGETABLES

The cooking method for all the following vegetables is steaming; if the vegetables are cooked in liquid, the times may vary. Green vegetables will be tender-crisp; root vegetables will be soft.

	PREP	MINUTES UNDER PRESSURE	PRESSURE	RELEASE
ACORN SQUASH	Halved	9	High	Quick
ARTICHOKES, LARGE	Whole	15	High	Quick
BEETS	Quartered if large; halved if small	9	High	Natural
BROCCOLI	Cut into florets	1	Low	Quick
BRUSSELS SPROUTS	Halved	2	High	Quick
BUTTERNUT SQUASH	Peeled, cut into ½-inch chunks	8	High	Quick
CABBAGE	Sliced	5	High	Quick
CARROTS	Cut into ½- to 1-inch slices	2	High	Quick
CAULIFLOWER	Whole	6	High	Quick
CAULIFLOWER	Cut into florets	1	Low	Quick
GREEN BEANS	Cut in halves or thirds	1	Low	Quick
SPAGHETTI SQUASH	Halved lengthwise	7	High	Quick

MEASUREMENT CONVERSION CHARTS

VOLUME EQUIVALENTS (LIQUID)

US STANDARD	US STANDARD (OUNCES)	METRIC (APPROXIMATE)
2 tablespoons	1 fl. oz.	30 mL
¼ cup	2 fl. oz.	60 mL
½ cup	4 fl. oz.	120 mL
1 cup	8 fl. oz.	240 mL
1½ cups	12 fl. oz.	355 mL
2 cups or 1 pint	16 fl. oz.	475 mL
4 cups or 1 quart	32 fl. oz.	1 L
1 gallon	128 fl. oz.	4 L

VOLUME EQUIVALENTS (DRY)

US STANDARD	METRIC (APPROXIMATE)
⅛ teaspoon	0.5 mL
¼ teaspoon	1 mL
½ teaspoon	2 mL
¾ teaspoon	4 mL
1 teaspoon	5 mL
1 tablespoon	15 mL
¼ cup	59 mL
⅓ cup	79 mL
½ cup	118 mL
⅔ cup	156 mL
¾ cup	177 mL
1 cup	235 mL
2 cups or 1 pint	475 mL
3 cups	700 mL
4 cups or 1 quart	1 L

OVEN TEMPERATURES

FAHRENHEIT (F)	CELSIUS (C) (APPROXIMATE)
250°	120°
300°	150°
325°	165°
350°	180°
375°	190°
400°	200°
425°	220°
450°	230°

WEIGHT EQUIVALENTS

US STANDARD	METRIC (APPROXIMATE)
½ ounce	15 g
1 ounce	30 g
2 ounces	60 g
4 ounces	115 g
8 ounces	225 g
12 ounces	340 g
16 ounces or 1 pound	455 g

RECIPE INDEX

INDEX

ACKNOWLEDGMENTS

I would like to thank the members of my Two Sleevers Facebook Group, for all the time you spend testing the recipes, for encouraging me and others, and—most of all—for making me laugh out loud daily as I read your comments. I look forward to chatting with you, and learning from you every day, for many years to come.

As always, my family continues to be my rock. I could not do half of everything I do without the support that my husband Roger provides daily, sometimes hourly. From helping me brainstorm, tasting everything I make, and setting up live videos, his contributions are integral to this book and to the blog.

Thank you to my son Alex, who will be leaving home for college soon, and whose presence and support I will miss dearly—not just because he helps with the dishes without complaining.

Thank you to my son Mark, who is missed at home and much-loved—I can't wait to cook all of the things for you.

I also want to thank all the wonderful people at Callisto Media, including Stacy Wagner-Kinnear, my editor. She is the reason why these cookbooks are well-structured, well-laid out, informative, and yet concise. I am grateful to Andrew Yackira for his editorial integrity and good humor, and to Janet Zimmerman and Michelle Anderson for their expertise. Finally, Sally Kim, Jenny Croghan, and Holly Smith have been a fantastic team, encouraging and supporting me every step of the way. Thank you for being my support.

I'd also like to thank Instant Pot®, and especially Anna Meglio, for their continued support and encouragement.